How Could She?

How Could She?

Dana Fowley

CENTURY · LONDON

Published by Century 2008

2 4 6 8 10 9 7 5 3 1

This book is a work of non-fiction based on the life, experiences and recollections of the author. In some limited cases dates, sequences or the detail of events have been changed to protect the privacy of others. The author has stated to the publishers that, except in such minor respects not affecting the substantial accuracy of the work, the contents of this book are true.

First published in Great Britain in 2008 byCentury
Random House, 20 Vauxhall Bridge Road,
London SW1V 2SA

www.rbooks.co.uk

Addresses for companies within The Random House Group Limited can be found at:
www.randomhouse.co.uk/offices.htm

The Random House Group Limited Reg. No. 954009

A CIP catalogue record for this book is available from the British Library

HB ISBN 9781846053863
TPB ISBN 9781846054570

The Random House Group Limited supports The Forest Stewardship Council (FSC), the leading international forest certification organisation. All our titles that are printed on Greenpeace approved FSC certified paper carry the FSC logo. Our paper procurement policy can be found at www.rbooks.co.uk/environment

Typeset in Spectrum MT by Palimpsest Book Production Limited,
Grangemouth, Stirlingshire
Printed and bound in Great Britain by CPI Mackays, Chatham ME5 8TD

This book is for my partner Paul, who has stood by me through everything, and for my sons Jordan and Dylan and my stepsons Paul and Ryan, who are my future. It is also for my sister Heather, who has helped me by just being there.

I also dedicate my story to all children who are now, or who have been, victims of child abuse. May they find the courage to stand up to their abusers, as I did.

Introduction

I heard only two words that the judge said.

'Twelve years.'

I looked at the woman in the dock, who stood there impassively, staring ahead. She showed no emotion.

As the words sank in, I slumped down in the hard seat of the public gallery in Edinburgh High Court. Uncontrollable sobs shook my body. Gail, my partner's sister-in-law, and Angela, the policewoman who has helped me through the last couple of terrible years, took me by my arms and half carried me out of the court. Outside in the foyer, I collapsed on one of the benches.

A firestorm of emotions raged through me. I was relieved and elated that three members of the gang of paedophiles who stole my childhood were going to spend a long time behind bars, but I was also riven with guilt. Because the woman with the long dark hair, who had just been sent down for twelve years, was my mother. And I, the principle witness against her, had put her in the dock.

The journey to that courtroom has been long and hard, and it started the day that I was born. What happened to me, at the hands of the person I should have been able to turn to for love and comfort, makes painful reading, but I'd like you to come on the journey with me because I believe my voice should be heard. Not just because it is my story, but because it is the story of hundreds of other children who have once suffered or continue to suffer at the hands of paedophiles.

The ring that abused me is the biggest ever to have come to justice in Britain. But that doesn't make it exceptional in its depravity. There are many more uncovered stories out there, hidden away by victims who can't face the shame or who are too terrified to bring their abusers to justice.

For many years, I, too, felt that I would rather bury the appalling memories of my childhood than confront those who were responsible. But with help and support from my partner Paul, I finally found the courage to seek justice. That is how I came to face my mother, whom I still love, across a courtroom.

Whenever anyone hears about my mum's major role in the horrific events of my childhood, they ask one question:

'How could she?'

It's a question I have asked many times, ever since I was old enough to understand what happened to me. I can't promise to answer it, I don't know that I, or anyone, will ever fully understand how any woman can be capable of such cruelty to her own child.

Today my mum is in prison and I am, for the first time in my life, really free. Writing this book has helped me come to terms with my own past. I'm one of the lucky ones: I have a home, children, and a happy life. Most victims of abuse don't have happy-ever-afters: they spend their lives in a twilight world of alcoholism, drug abuse, prostitution – anything to escape from themselves.

It is for them that I am writing this. I want the world to know what my life was like, and I want other victims to feel empowered by me.

1

My mum married my dad on the most romantic day of the year, Valentine's Day. It was 1980 and it was also the day of her sixteenth birthday. Instead of a wedding dress she wore a maternity smock because she was heavily pregnant with me – I was born just four months later. It wasn't a shotgun wedding, because nobody was holding a gun to my dad's head. He was happy to marry her. But the only romance in their relationship was the date they married: he soon discovered that the reality of marriage didn't agree with him. Mum's family were dead against the match. Pregnant or not, they didn't want her to marry him.

Mum, whose name was Caroline Dunsmore before she married my dad, Tam Fowley, had been living at home with my granddad and nana before the wedding, but she and Tam had their own council flat by the time I was born. They'd met because my mum was friends with Tam's sister Sheena.

Fifteen months after I was born, my sister Heather followed me into the world. We moved around a lot – my mum has spent her whole life moving from one flat to another, never staying in one place for long. I don't know why she moved so much, no doubt a psychiatrist would find some meaningful reason for it hidden deep in her own troubled childhood. I don't think it was due to rent arrears, because the council was always her landlord, wherever she moved. And it wasn't as though we ever moved very far: there are two pages of the Edinburgh street directory which encompass my whole childhood, apart from one brief stay in the countryside. I attended five different primary schools, but, with one exception, they are all within a few square miles of each other.

Were they ever happily married? I doubt it. Certainly, by the time I was old enough to be aware of anything, the constant sound in our home was of the two of them arguing. Tam was a drunken bully. He was nine years older than Mum, and much taller than her. She's small, like me, so her slightly built frame was no match for him. He was handy with his fists, as they say, and all three of us felt the brunt of his temper from time to time. It wasn't so much that he would hit me and Heather, but he was abruptly forceful and rough with us, and we had good reason to be frightened of him. For example, without warning he would grab us and force us to sit up straight. We would sit like two little petrified statues, not speaking, not moving. Mum was never able to stop him, and I don't think she ever really tried. I don't remember Dad ever having a job, as he was around the house all the time. I soon came to realise that the distinctive smell on his breath was the stench of alcohol: the biggest love affair of Dad's life at that time was with Tennent's lager.

I have few memories of my dad from those early days. But I do remember one day when, while Mum was out, he had another woman in the house. He took her into a different room from us and, although I didn't see anything, I now know that he wanted to be alone with her, not bothered by two small girls. He told me and Heather to sit on the settee, and when I asked to go to the toilet he said, 'Sit up, don't move, or I'll smack you.' I started to cry, scared because I was desperate to go to the toilet. I was only three years old, and I didn't know what to do.

'And if you wet yourself you'll get smacked even harder,' he shouted. In the end, after trying with all my might to hold it, I had to give in and wet myself. I was too terrified to move, and sat there hoping that Mum would be home soon. It's such a distant memory that I don't know what happened when she did get home.

I know that at times she was scared of him too. Sometimes he would burn her on the face and legs with his cigarette, and once he attacked her with a hammer. So she most likely didn't even challenge him about why I'd wet myself.

As I grew up I heard other stories about my dad which made my blood run cold. Before I was born, Mum told me that when he crashed the car, he rescued himself and his mother from the wreckage, but left my heavily pregnant mum in there. I was told that when I was six weeks old he tried to suffocate me with a pillow, because, according to Mum, he was jealous of the attention I was getting. On one occasion, according to my nana, he held Mum over a balcony with an axe in his hand, and he said he would chop her up, so that Nana could have half and he could have half. I was also told by my Auntie Sheena, his sister, that once he slapped me across the face so hard that it left a red imprint of his hand on my cheek.

These are other people's memories, but one of the most vivid of my own is of the night Dad left home. I was lying in bed, listening to another vicious fight between him and Mum, when the door suddenly slammed and the flat went unusually silent. Looking back, you'd think the peace would have been a relief, but it wasn't. I cried and cried for him that night, lying next to Mum, who had taken me into her bed. She didn't shed a single tear: she was glad he had gone.

Worse was to come. We soon discovered he'd moved in with a woman who lived across the road. The woman had a little girl roughly the same age as me, and I remember seeing him walking along the road holding hands with his new 'daughter'. Every time he went past I'd cry for him. There was a low wall outside the flats opposite, and I used to walk along it and shout for my dad. If I saw his new woman I'd call out:

'You stole my daddy.'

Sometimes he'd come back, but he never stayed for long.

Always, when he reappeared, he would put on the Cliff Richard record 'Daddy's Home'. He would promise me he was back for good – but very soon, usually after only a few hours, he'd be off again. Even today, if I ever catch, by chance, a few bars of that song, I feel tears pricking my eyes. If he had stayed would my life have been better? Who knows. We were, by anyone's reckoning, a low-class family. My dad drank, he was violent; my life would never have been good, but it might not have been as savagely cruel as it turned out to be.

After he'd gone, my mum continued to take Heather and me to visit his mother, our granny. She still treated us as her grandchildren, although even that relationship soured when Tam turned up one day while we were visiting. I ran excitedly towards him, but he brushed me aside to pick up the little girl of his new partner, the 'new daughter' who had taken my place, to introduce her to my granny. She was welcomed with arms wide open. I hated her: she had taken my daddy, and I had to come to terms with the fact that he would never come back. Before too long, Mum had divorced him, and she gave a statement about his violence to the court.

We lived on benefits, and never had enough money for clothes and the bills. But as a child I was never aware of poverty: in the area where we lived, our circumstances were normal. Muirhouse is a rough, tough area of Edinburgh, but back then it was all I knew, and it had everything we needed. There was a large parade of shops just a few minutes' walk away and there was a park with swings where we played.

Now that my life has moved on so far, when I drive through those streets I know that no money in the world would persuade me to live there again. But when I grew up and left the area I really missed it. It's true you had to watch your back as you walked to the shops, but it's also true that by the time you got to them you'd have stopped loads of times to answer the question: 'How are you, hen?' There was a friendship, a kinship, which I missed when I first moved to a better-off area. Everybody knew you in Muirhouse. Now, of course, I see it through different eyes; I notice the girls who are pregnant before they are old enough to leave school, the druggies, the drunks, the street fights.

We must have been struggling at times, because I remember one Christmas Mum had nothing, no presents for us, no special meal. Nana came to the rescue and paid for our entire Christmas: the tree, decorations, all our presents, and an all-the-trimmings Christmas lunch at her house.

I can't remember the dates of Tam's comings and goings any more, but by the time of their third wedding anniversary, Mum's nineteenth birthday, he and she were estranged, although at some point that year I'm sure they had another of their brief reunions. On that day Mum was given a birthday present by her father and a friend of his: a night of sex with a young man they knew, who was the same age as she was. I heard about this from Mum herself, years later. You might think that's a strange present for a father to give his daughter, but that's because you don't yet know my family.

I don't imagine the night of passion was the great success my granddad hoped it would be, because Mum and the young man never became an item. But the pal of my granddad's who helped set up the birthday present was the one who really made a big hit with my mum. His name was Billy King and he was over twenty years older than Mum, but within months they had moved in together. He became my stepfather, and lived with us for the next eleven years, marrying Mum after they had been together six or seven years.

I first met Billy at Nana and Granddad's house. He was there with Mum, and although it was clear he was a friend of Granddad's, I somehow sensed straightaway that he was with Mum in a romantic way. They were laughing and joking, and he was talking very nicely to me and Heather, asking us questions about ourselves, patting us on the head, complimenting Mum on how well behaved and pretty we were.

Soon after that first meeting, we all moved into a two-floor flat in May Court, just off Pennywell Medway, which is the first home I can remember clearly. It was only a five-minute walk from our last flat. May Court is a large four-storey grey block with two communal stairways, and our flat was on the second floor with internal stairs up to the two bedrooms: one for me and Heather, one for Billy and Mum.

Billy was a short, fat man. Not just a bit fat, really fat, weighing more than twenty stone. He wore glasses and had dark receding hair, with a bald patch on top. There was nothing physically attractive about him, and it was hard to see why Mum was so taken with him. But in those early days he seemed like good news for our family. He had an ice-cream van which he drove around the area selling ice cream from and he often brought sweets and chocolate home for us. He always dressed smartly, and he was out all day working, which was a novelty, as not many members of my family worked, and he was always generous with the money he had.

I remember him and Mum taking me and Heather on a day trip to Burntisland, a small seaside town on the Firth of Forth. There was a funfair, and we went on a few rides. They bought us ice cream and silly, colourful wigs. I thought it was great. We played with buckets and spades making sandcastles on the beach. I wanted to go in the sea, but I was scared that I would be bitten by a crab or some other sea creature, so Mum and Billy each held me by one hand and took me down to the water's edge, trying to coax me to paddle. I was only four, but I can remember lying in bed that night feeling that I would burst with happiness.

That was the nearest we ever came to having a holiday, and it is etched in my memory because it was one of the few, truly happy days of my childhood. If you were to ask me for good memories, there are very few before the age of seventeen. It's as if my life has been made up of two distinct parts. If there were good times in my childhood, I think they have been overwhelmed by everything else that happened, to me, and suffocated by my memories of the bad times. I can't revive many of the good times, just Burntisland, that tiny fragment of normal family life, and a few other hazy recollections of brief escapes from what became the enduring nightmare of my childhood.

Mum never showed any love or affection for me and Heather. We were never cuddled or told we were loved. If we fell over, she never ran to pick us up, or soothe us when we cut our knees or bruised our legs. To us this was normal, and you can't miss what you have never known. She kept the house clean and tidy, we were always washed and well dressed, and she cooked proper meals for us. Outwardly, she was a good mum. She was of low intelligence – she'd been sent to a special school for children with learning difficulties when she was young – but she was certainly bright enough to run a home.

The only real love that was shown towards me came from Mum's sister, Auntie Brenda. Mum was the oldest of three children, and Brenda was the youngest. She was only twelve when I was born, and she adored having a baby to look after and play with. Even in her teens, I was still her favourite, and she spent hours looking after me and Heather.

I can remember when I was five, on my first day at school, I was dressed in my crisp, new uniform, clutching a smart new school bag and Brenda took a photograph of me. She came with Mum to take me to school, and we walked along the road, me holding her hand, and her with tears running down her cheeks because I was going to be away all day.

Within weeks of that happy little picture, my real childhood began. The childhood which I had to battle hard to claw my way out of, and which only now I am beginning to put to rest.

I was at home in the flat alone with Billy, just a few months after my fifth birthday. When he walked into the living room where I was on the settee, watching TV, I had no reason not to trust him. Until that moment he had always been friendly, he'd never hit me, and he'd always been generous with us. Unlike Mum, he knew how to express affection, he would occasionally praise us for being well behaved, and he always said goodnight to us. But suddenly he was standing in front of me, opening his trousers. He grabbed my head in both hands and forced me to perform oral sex on him. It was so shocking I didn't have a chance to resist, and I wouldn't have been able to overcome his strength anyway. I had no understanding of what was happening: I was terrified and confused. I had never seen a man's body before. I was horrified by the sight, the smell, the enormity of him in my mouth. I was gagging and heaving and tears were running down my face. It seemed to last for ages, and when he climaxed in my mouth I was sick. He wiped my face with a towel. I was crying and still heaving, but he casually said, 'Go and play in your room.' Then he shouted after me, almost as an afterthought, 'Don't tell anybody.'

He was calm and acted so normal. I ran to my room,

crying and still throwing up, not knowing what had happened, not knowing it was wrong, but knowing that I hated it. I lay on my bed and sobbed for what seemed like hours. When Mum came home with Heather, the rest of the day was perfectly normal, and Billy behaved as though nothing had happened. This normality, this ability to switch from scenes of depravity to routine domesticity, would become very familiar to me over the years to come. It was the hallmark of the abuse that continued unchecked and never mentioned in my own family home.

I didn't tell Mum. He had told me not to. I was five years old and I did exactly as I was told. I didn't know what else I could or should do. I'd never been frightened of Billy before, but I was now. It wouldn't have made any difference if I had told Mum, because obviously he actually shared it with her. How does a man tell the woman he is living with that he has abused her five-year-old daughter? I have often wondered how he broached the subject, what he said. He must have been fairly confident that for some reason she did not regard child abuse with the horror the rest of society would. Even so, I'd like to know the words he used when he told her what he had done to me. I can't imagine any mother, apart from her, calmly accepting that a man had abused her daughter. I'd want to kill any man who told me he had touched my children, and I think my reaction is the normal one. But I know her well enough now to be able to say how she reacted: coldly and without any disapproval. He didn't have to threaten her or cajole her. She accepted it, willingly.

I know that he told her, because the following day was the start of their unholy alliance.

When I got home from school the next day I was so relieved to see that my mum was in. I thought he wouldn't dare touch me again if Mum was there. She would protect me. She would keep me safe.

But she looked at me with strangely cold eyes, and ordered me to come through into the living room.

'Take your trousers off,' she said.

'No, Mum, no . . .' I wailed, sobs choking my voice as the realisation that something unknown was about to happen sunk in. In the living room I could see Billy lying on the floor, his lower half undressed.

'Do as you are told,' she said, her voice harsh. I looked at her with fear and confusion, but she didn't look at me. Instead, after I miserably pulled off my clothes, she lifted me and placed me on top of him. I tried to cling to her, but she pulled my arms from round her neck and forced me down on to him.

The pain of him penetrating me was agonising, and I struggled to force myself off him, but she held me down. I was begging him to stop and telling Mum how much it hurt, with tears coursing down my face. I felt I was being ripped apart, and terrible, searing-hot pain spread from between my legs through my stomach. Mum held me in place, and when I turned to look into her face she gave me a cold stare. There was no pity in her face, and I felt incredibly alone. I can still remember that feeling: it was one of complete desolation.

The ordeal seemed to last for a long time. My whole body convulsed with agony, but the more I screamed the more she shouted: 'Do as you are told! Keep quiet.'

This time he had full sex with me. I had no idea what was happening, what he was doing, why I had to be tortured like this. I was terrified, not just of the pain, but of the awful look on Billy's face, which was flushed and contorted.

After it was over my mother handed me my clothes and I heard the words that became such a familiar repetition: 'Go to your room and play.'

Climbing the stairs was agony, and I put my hand between my legs to hold back the pain, but it gave me very little relief. Each step hurt, and it took me ages to reach the top of the stairs. When I got to my room I lay on my bed sobbing. When I moved my hand from between my legs I was terrified to see it was covered in blood. I didn't know what to do; I didn't dare go downstairs and tell anybody. I thought I was going to die.

Eventually I cried myself to sleep, and when I woke the pain had eased off a bit. I put my clothes on and tentatively made my way downstairs, taking each step carefully. In the living room, everything looked so normal. Mum and Billy were drinking tea, and Heather was playing on the floor with her toys. Mum and Billy turned to look at me as I walked in and I remember all Mum said was, 'We'll be having dinner soon.'

I nodded and slowly walked across to the settee to watch television with them.

I didn't dare mention the pain, and they both acted as if nothing had happened. After dinner Mum went upstairs to run our bath. She told me I was getting in first, which was unusual because Heather and I were usually bathed together. When I took my clothes off they were stained with my blood, but Mum said nothing. Climbing into the hot water was terribly painful, enough to take my breath away. I cried, but no notice was taken; still Mum said nothing. I was dried and Mum put my pyjamas on, and then I had to make the long painful journey down the stairs again. Mum took Heather for her bath and I sat in silence on the settee with Billy. He said, 'Did you get your bath?'

I said yes, and then we watched the TV screen in silence. I was scared: I wanted Mum and Heather to come back, but it seemed to take a long time before they were downstairs again. Heather wanted me to play with her, but I was in too much pain to move, and eventually I made my way slowly up the stairs to bed. I stuffed my face into the pillow to muffle the sound of my crying, so that Heather would not hear.

The pattern of my childhood had been set that day: from now on there was no escape. My mother, the person who should have nurtured and protected me, was in on everything.

The pain lasted for several days, and was particularly bad when I went to the toilet, when the burning sensation almost made me faint. I tried hard to forget it, but eventually I told Mum. Her reply was, 'It will be OK.' She didn't give me anything for the pain, not even a cuddle.

That was the beginning, and in some ways it was the worst thing that happened. Although I was to be subjected to far more horrifying and painful ordeals, this experience has always stood out because it was the first time I realised that I couldn't even trust my own mother to protect me. Until then, she had been all right as a mother: not cuddly or affectionate, but all right. I had no idea until that day how cold she was. It was her betrayal that allowed everything that followed to happen, and the betrayal of a child by their mother is the most unnatural thing in the world. If she had protected me, my life story would have been very different. The day she helped Billy abuse me laid down a marker: from then on, I was fair game for any paedophile.

2

After that first rape, it happened all the time. Billy had sex with me, or forced me to have oral sex, on a regular basis, whether Mum was there or not. I constantly lived in fear of him. It always made me feel sick, and I never got used to it. Although he took a pride in his appearance, he was fat and sweaty, so he was often smelly, which made my urge to gag even stronger. When Mum was there, she would still lift me on to him and hold me down, and I soon learned to stop pleading with her to help me, because all she ever gave me was her stoney glare and a few emotionless commands: 'Take your clothes off. Come here. Stop making that noise.'

Heather was never there when it happened, and to this day she insists they never abused her. I think it was a clever ploy on Mum and Billy's part: if I had said anything to anyone, Heather wouldn't have been able to back me up, and I wouldn't have been believed. Or perhaps Heather has simply blanked those memories. Maybe, in some twisted way, I served Billy's depraved urges better than she did.

Every time it was over I heard the same carefree, dismissive words: 'Away you go and play' or 'Off you go to your games.'

Then Mum would ask Billy if he wanted a cup of tea, and get busy making the mince and tatties or fish fingers and chips for our tea, for all the world as though nothing had happened. I'd lie on my bed listening to them laughing and giggling together. They never rowed, not like Mum and Dad had. They were a strong couple; they were made for each other in many ways you could never imagine. After a while, when I realised it was going to carry on happening, I cried less, and only from the physical pain – the numbing sense of isolation and betrayal was constantly with me. I would do what they said, and within minutes of it happening I would be able to blank it from my mind and go back to playing with my toys. I learned that the sooner I could shut myself off to the abuse, the better I could cope with it all. Eventually, it became so routine to me that my recovery time was very fast. I accepted the brutal rapes as part and parcel of normal, everyday life.

Apart from the abuse my life felt pretty normal. We were well looked after, well fed, clean, well dressed, and we got on OK. Mum and Billy were not drinkers and they rarely went out, so there was no shortage of money. No teacher would have singled me out as a child from a problem family, no social workers ever came knocking at our door, and we never had cause for a policeman to arrive on our doorstep.

In a way, that made it all so much harder. It would have been easier to just have hated them. If my life had been all bad, I wouldn't have so many mixed emotions now about my mum. If she had never allowed the abuse to start she might not have been the most loving of mums, but she would have been a mum, just a normal mum. That is all any child wants, all I have ever wanted.

Soon after Billy moved in, Heather started calling him 'Dad'. She was younger than me, and I don't think she had any memories of our real dad, so it was easy for her. It took me longer: I think he had been living with us for about a year before I called him 'Dad'. It happened, I suppose, because everyone around us, including my mum, referred to him as my dad. In the eyes of the world (eyes that were not privy to the appalling sexual abuse that was going on behind our closed door) they were good parents. They appeared to play an active role in our well-being. Mum went to some of my school parents' evenings, Billy even helped with my homework when I was older.

Although, in those early years, I went to a succession of different schools, I was a regular attender. I liked school, and I did well there. Thanks to Billy's income I always had money for school outings and I was always tidily dressed. In the early days, when Billy had his ice-cream van, he always gave us treats. Later, when he no longer had the van, if another ice-cream van came into our street he'd send us out to buy lollies and ice creams. OK, we never had foreign holidays, but we had everything the other kids living around us had. Billy would buy us a good Christmas too and when we were a bit older, Mum would take us up the town to choose new clothes for Christmas.

Billy did his share at home, as well as working and providing the money. Although Mum did all the cleaning and washing, he helped out with the cooking. Although he was grossly fat, he ate sensibly – he wasn't stuffing himself with sweets and chocolate, and he was the one who made sure we ate fresh vegetables and fruit. His weight problem was related to the fact that he was an insulin-dependent diabetic. In fact, whenever we had good meals, Billy was the one who cooked them. Mum was OK at opening packets and shoving things like fish fingers and chips in the oven, but Billy knew how to do casseroles and stews, and he would regularly make a big pot of soup that would last a few days. Every Sunday morning, he always cooked us all a big fried breakfast, without fail, and during the week he'd make porridge. When it came to doing a roast dinner, he and Mum would both be in the kitchen sharing the work.

Billy and Mum didn't take us out to eat or to the cinema. But I can remember Auntie Brenda taking me to see a rerun of *E.T.* when I was about six. It was my first time in a cinema, which was a bit overwhelming, but what I remember most of all is crying my eyes out at the story.

I was always given birthday presents, just as other children are, although I don't ever remember being taken out for a birthday treat or having a birthday party. I don't think that was unusual, as I don't recall going to anyone else's birthday parties either. I do remember pestering for a pair of roller skates, and on my next birthday they were there. And I have clear memories of two dolls, one with a leather skirt, and another one that looked like a baby.

When we were little, Heather and I got on well and often played together with our dolls; although, I guess like all little sisters, she had a habit of whining to Mum or Billy if she thought I wasn't giving her a fair share of anything. She was a real little grass: it was always 'Mum, Dana's not sharing with me', or, if we broke something, she would pipe up straight away with, 'Dana did it.' We'd get told off for squabbling, but no more than any other children.

I had a good friend I played with as well, a girl called Michelle, who lived in one of the other flats in May Court. We'd push our dolls in their prams around the pathways and grassy areas surrounding the block. I'd go to her home and she'd come to mine: Mum and Billy would be perfect parents while she was there. I instinctively knew they wouldn't abuse me while she was there: they were far too careful when strangers were around.

Billy and Mum weren't obviously affectionate towards each other: I never saw them hug or kiss or hold hands. But he never shouted at her and he was never violent towards her or us when we were at home. Billy was good to her, I cannot deny that. What did he get in return? He got me, he got the right to do anything he wanted with me. I reckon he thought it was a pretty good trade-off.

So there was some normality in my life, but it is hard for me to dredge those memories up. What they did to me was so huge, so overwhelming, that it pushed the good memories down deep.

The abuse soon escalated and my mum became increasingly involved. Billy would come to my bedroom at night. He always knocked on the door, I don't know why: looking back, it seems a very unusual gesture of politeness in a way of life where no consideration was ever given to me. He never waited to be told to come in. If we were living in a flat where I had to share a room with Heather, he'd pull me out of bed and take me into the next room, where he and Mum would have sex with me. She took an active part and he would direct me in what he wanted me to do, to both her and himself.

It didn't happen every night. It's hard now to quantify how often it was, because in my memory so many nights have blurred together. It was probably three or four times a week. Sometimes I would already have fallen asleep, but often I would be lying there, rigid with fear, dreading the knock and praying that this would be one of the nights it didn't come. There were televisions in every room, and I would listen for the sound of the one in the living room being turned off and the one in their bedroom going on: that meant they were going to bed. Then I'd hold my breath and pray this was one of the nights they would just go to sleep.

I used to believe Heather was Billy's favourite, but I think that was simply because he didn't abuse her. He didn't favour her in other ways, she wasn't spoiled with sweets or anything. I never resented her; I just accepted it. And if she ever noticed that I was treated differently, what could she have done? There was no one to help me and soon there would be no one to help either of us.

Terrible as it was, the abuse I suffered at the hands of Billy and Mum would soon become one of the easier crosses I had to bear. Pain and suffering, I know from experience, are relative. Billy and Mum abused me at our own home, but what happened elsewhere was unbearable in comparison.

The House of Hell is an ordinary-looking three-bedroomed, pebble-dashed semi, fronted by a wall with small black iron railings which hems in the tiny front garden. The only distinctive feature is its next-door neighbour: it stands right against the boundary of a big electronic engineering factory (known locally as Ferranti's, although in fact the Ferranti company was sold in the 1990s and the business is now owned by Marconi). A nine-foot-high steel fence encloses the factory site, giving it a slightly menacing appearance. Yet for me, the menace is all on the outside of the fence, in that innocuous-looking ex-council house. Even today, fifteen years after I was last inside the house, just looking at it from the road makes me shiver. The front door is painted a different colour, the blinds at the window have changed. But it is still the place where I, and my sister Heather, suffered abuse that is off the scale of human depravity.

Billy's parents, Granddad and Nana King, lived in the House of Hell, which is the name I gave it when I was old enough to know that what happened there was deeply wrong. They were my step-grandparents and I knew them as Granddad and Nana King. They were in their early sixties when I was first introduced to them. It was Billy who took me, without Mum and Heather, to their house in Muirhouse Green for the first time. I was six years old by this time and the abuse at home had been going on for months. He put me in his car and drove me round there, a journey of less than five minutes. He didn't tell me where we were going or why, but something in his manner made me afraid.

When we got there, there were no happy introductions, nobody even spoke to me, ruffled their hand through my hair or made a fuss of me. I thought nothing of how strange it all was: it was only later that I came to realise how unnatural my childhood was. I just stood shyly in the kitchen while Billy spoke to his parents.

Then my new 'grandmother' thrust a cup into my hands and ordered me to drink: whenever Heather and I were taken there, we were always given a cup of cola or some other fizzy drink as soon as we arrived, whether we were thirsty or not. They insisted we drank it. With hindsight, I can guess that the drinks were spiked with drugs, probably to make us drowsy, although I don't remember whether it made me sleepy. On one occasion Nana King gave me a small white tablet to swallow, and that really did make me feel groggy. I know that Granddad King was prescribed heart medication by his doctor, so perhaps it was one of his heart tablets.

After my drink in the kitchen, Granddad and Nana King went upstairs, and Billy said, 'Go on, up you go.' He nodded towards the stairs, and I went up. He came up behind me. I can remember the layout of that house vividly, as over the years of my childhood, I was taken there so often. The stairs were straight ahead from the door into the kitchen, and when we reached the top he put his hand on my shoulder and directed me across the horseshoe-shaped landing to the room I would come to know and dread. It was Granddad and Nana King's bedroom, and every corner and crevice of that room is deeply impressed on my memory. There were large old wooden wardrobes along one wall, and bedside tables at each side of the double bed. As I lay on the bed, the window was straight ahead, with slatted horizontal blinds which were always closed. The curtains were white, with flowers on them. I used to stare at those flowers, so incongruously bright and pretty, to help me through the dire days I spent there.

I am not going to go into detail about the abuse. I have thought about this long and hard, and know that I don't want this book to become a handbook for paedophiles, a manual to titillate and inspire their horrible crimes. God forgive me if any child suffers because I have chosen to be open and honest about what happened to me. I believe that by telling my story I am helping to shed light on this taboo subject, but I don't want to be in any way guilty of encouraging crimes, or even fantasies, that involve children.

But to understand my life you must have a brief glimpse of my agony, however unpalatable.

Everyone was involved. Granddad King was, to me, an old man, with white, receding hair, glasses and a beer gut. He was not as fat as his son Billy, but he was a big man. He always wore proper trousers, never jeans or tracksuit bottoms. Nana King was old and frail-looking, very skinny with thin grey hair. She did not look like the fairytale version of a granny, and she certainly wasn't. There was a hard glint in her eyes. She was as deeply involved as each of the men, and there were no boundaries between them – everyone in that room stripped naked and had sex in some shape or form with the others and with me. The only one not willingly participating was me. I was six years old. What could I do?

After it was over I was told to put my pants and trousers back on and go downstairs. They would all call after me:

'Remember – don't tell anyone.'

'You'll be in serious trouble if you do.'

'They'll take you away.'

They followed me downstairs and all sat around in the living room talking about normal things, as if Billy and I had just popped in for a family visit. Again, the absurd normality of the room, with a line-up of family photos on the walls, and a huge fish tank, jarred with me. I sat in a corner of the settee, rigid and silent, but unquestioning. It happened to me at home, now it was happening to me here. I hated it, but I accepted it because I didn't know anything else.

For the next six years, until the death of Granddad King, the House of Hell became a regular part of my life, and Heather's too. Although Mum and Billy never abused Heather at home, she was taken up there for Granddad and Nana King to abuse – although whenever she was there, Mum and Billy would not come in. I have never really worked that out. They were not protecting her: they certainly knew what was happening to her, it was the only reason that we were taken there. We were forced to perform sex acts on each other and also on Nana King, as well as on the men. On one occasion, Granddad King put us together in the bath and urinated over us, and on another he thrust a toothbrush inside us 'to clean you properly'.

Don't think for a minute that Mum was 'left out', or that she simply colluded in the abuse. She may not have been there on my introduction to the House of Hell, but she was a regular participant in the grossly abusive group sex that went on there whenever it was just me, not Heather. Over those six years I guess I was forced to go there literally hundreds of times. It was not a regular pattern, but it was more than once a week. The worst words I ever heard were 'We're going to Granddad and Nana King's.' Just writing them now, all these years on, makes me convulse with fear. Then we would be bundled into the car. If Mum met anyone as we went to the car she'd say, 'Just taking Dana to see Billy's mum and dad.'

It sounded so normal, so nice; a little girl being taken to visit her grandparents. I hated those car journeys. Even though it only took minutes, it was long enough to anticipate what was going to happen. By the time we arrived, I would be almost paralysed with fear. Later, having moved several times, we came to live near to them, and I would be told to go up there on my own. I never dared to disobey, but I can remember knocking at that door, and my heart would be beating so loudly with fear that I could hear it in my ears. I knew I was on my own, that my mum was not going to save me, and there was nobody else I could turn to.

What made the abuse at the House of Hell so much worse than anywhere else was that it involved sadistic violence. Granddad and Nana King rivalled each other in their capacity for evil, but he was probably marginally ahead, if only because he was bigger and stronger and could inflict more damage. One of his favourite tricks was to partially throttle me while he was raping me from behind. He would hold my throat, pressing down on my windpipe. My memory of the feeling of panic as my breathing was cut off and I gasped for air is still physically overwhelming today: my face flushes and I feel my blood race through my veins as I think about it. I can remember the sensation of coughing and spluttering, and the room spinning and my head feeling tight, just before I blacked out completely, and then came to on the floor. Nobody was worried: they weren't clustered around to see if I was all right. The orgy was continuing around me.

I passed out many times, either from pain or, I suppose, as my body's defence mechanism to get me away from what was happening.

Granddad King did this same throttling trick on Heather, and I believe that he may well be responsible for permanent damage to her. When the brain is starved of oxygen it starts to shut down. If the oxygen supply comes back immediately, there is no damage. But even a few seconds too long, and brain function can be harmed.

Heather has learning difficulties, and for much of her childhood she attended a special school. But until she was about eight, she was in normal school; she used to come to school with me. I can't prove that Granddad King's savagery robbed her of some of her mental ability, but it is what I believe happened. Her brain, I think, was starved of oxygen while that animal of a man was deliberately suffocating her.

Today, Heather can read and write at a standard equivalent to that of a twelve-year-old. But her understanding of the world is that of an even younger child. She lives with me, and her life is now happy and fulfilled, but her journey has been longer and perhaps even more difficult than mine. At times, I think it is a good thing that she does not understand more about what happened to her, but at other times I think that if the damage had not been done to her brain, perhaps she would have escaped earlier.

Granddad and Nana King used to tie us up with belts as well. I remember them tying me and Heather together round our legs, and with our hands behind our backs. Heather was crying and I desperately wanted to cry, too, but I fought it with all my might, because I knew that the more upset I was, the worse Heather would be. Even today, as a grown woman, she takes her cue from me, and if I'm unhappy, she's unhappy. I kept telling her she would be all right. After leaving us tied together for what seemed like ages, Granddad King would untie me and throw me on to the bed to have sex with me. I would feel relief because he was leaving Heather alone, but it was short-lived because when he had finished with me he would start on her. I think I was about eight or nine when this happened, and Heather just a year younger.

Today, I still feel guilty when I remember my ambivalent attitude to Heather being abused. On the one hand I always wanted them to take the worst out on me and spare her, but on the other hand, my instinct for self-preservation meant that I would hope that they would take her, not me. It made no difference what you wished for: it was always both of us, either one by one or together.

Routinely, after they had finished their sex games, they would whip us with the belts, hard enough to take my breath away and make me cry out in agony. Mum and Billy, who never attacked me physically in their own home, would join in at the House of Hell. In fact, Mum was often the prime mover. It was as if she wanted to prove she could hurt me even more than anyone else. I would be tied by my hands to the headboard of the bed with a belt, and then she'd lash me with another belt, showing the others where to hit me to hurt me most. Then she'd pass the belt to one of the others, and they'd take it in turns.

Even on occasions when it looked as if I wasn't going to be beaten, and I was hoping to scurry away with only the pain of the sexual abuse to deal with, she'd initiate it.

She wanted to please them, to show them it was OK to rape and beat us, to do whatever they wanted with her daughters.

I remember thinking that one day she would let them kill me. I think she would have done, if that was what they had wanted.

When they were beating me it was impossible not to cry, although I tried my best not to: it seemed that the more you cried and whimpered, the more pleasure they got and the longer the beating would last. I would tense my body and screw my eyes tightly closed, holding my breath, but as the blows struck I would be forced to cry out. The pain was so intense that I could hardly breathe, and where the belt had lashed into me my body would be stinging and hot, often for days afterwards. Sometimes the skin broke and I bled, but my wounds were never covered. Getting dressed after these ordeals was agonising.

Looking back, perhaps they timed the abuse for when they knew the neighbours would not be in, otherwise I'm sure my screams would have been heard. I can remember both Billy and Nana King snarling at me to 'keep the noise down', probably worried that passers-by would hear me. Granddad King sometimes put his hand over my mouth, but at other times they just let me scream. They were also clever enough to keep the beating where the marks wouldn't show, on my trunk, my buttocks, the tops of my legs.

Usually the whipping, which would bring large red wheals up all over our bodies (it happened to Heather, too), would happen after sex, but not always. When we arrived at the house we would often be sent into the garden to play, and then called in, usually one at a time, for the abuse. It was impossible to play as we waited: the gnawing anticipation of pain made me feel sick, and terror took away any inclination for toys and games.

Unlike Billy and Mum, who were normal the rest of the time when they weren't abusing me, there was nothing redeeming about Granddad and Nana King. Once, soon after we arrived and before anything sexual had happened, Heather asked if she could have 'a piece with margarine' (a Scottish expression for a slice of bread). She was whipped with a belt by Granddad King just for asking. If there were other people there to witness them, they would be quite nice to us, giving us money to get ice creams from the ice-cream van. But they never took us out, never talked to us. And these treats were always for other people's eyes: we were never given anything unless outsiders were present.

The worst physical attack I suffered was when I was sent to the House of Hell when Granddad King was on his own. He had sex with me, and then he started beating me with a poker. The poker was a familiar instrument of torture in that house: on more than one occasion the four of them, Granddad and Nana King, Billy and Mum, had taken turns thrusting it up my backside, which is one of the most painful things I can ever remember. I was face down on the bed, and I remember crying out: 'Please stop, I'll do anything if you stop!'

'We're not going to stop. It's your fault. You know it's your fault. You want us to do this,' said Granddad King.

This was Granddad King's speciality, mental torture. He would always taunt me after the orgy was over. 'You know it's your fault that we're doing this, don't you?'; 'You're making us do this; You're a dirty little girl, aren't you? You're asking for this, aren't you?'

I always agreed with him. If I had disagreed, I'd have been given another beating. Besides, for all I knew, perhaps it was my own fault. I had never been told what I did that was so terrible to deserve this life, but I was too young to have any resources to question it. If he said it was my fault, it was my fault. All I knew was that I hated it and I wanted it to stop.

The day he beat me with the poker was probably the most savage and out of control attack I ever suffered. I had started to go downstairs after the sex, and he followed me out of the bedroom and lashed out at me, over and over again. I cowered, whimpering, with my hands above my head to stave off the blows. My body was later covered with bruises, particularly my sides, back, and the tops of my legs, and my wrists were black from trying to protect myself. Suddenly he stopped, and within seconds he had calmed down and told me to go. He didn't check to see if I was all right. I couldn't leave straightaway, because I knew I had to stop crying before I could go out into the street. I sat on the stairs, until I could get my sobs in check. He was in the living room, watching the television as if nothing had happened. He didn't speak to me, and after a few minutes I let myself quietly out and went home, trying not to limp and wince too much with the pain.

When I got home, for the first time ever Mum and Billy showed some concern. Not for me, but for the fact that the bruising might be spotted by someone outside the family. They didn't take me to a doctor or give me any painkillers. I was told to tell anybody who asked that I had been playing on the school roof and had fallen off. I think it must have been during a school holiday, because no staff at school noticed it. When one of my friends saw my wrists, I dutifully repeated the lie about the school roof.

Nana King was equally cruel. She would also verbally abuse me while they were all having sex with me. She would call me 'a dirty little cow' and ask me 'Do you want it?' as she forced me to commit some obscene sex act. I said 'aye', because to say 'no' was to ask for an even more vicious beating at the end. She would use the belt to hit me and Heather and, for a frail old lady, she could lash very hard.

I never talked about what was happening to me, never told anyone outside the family. They, my abusers, told me not to tell, and I was frightened and always did what I was told. It was a very normal part of my life, it happened to me all the time, but some instinct told me, even when I was very young, that it was not normal for other people, not something to talk about – although I do remember that for a while, when I was very young, I assumed it happened in every family. When you are as young as I was when it started, just five years old, you accept everything your parents tell you or give you. Your home is the boundary of your life. I was moulded into thinking what happened to me was normal. I had no other choice but to live that life.

As I got older the actual physical process of being sexually abused became less painful, although it never stopped hurting. But I also became more and more aware that it wasn't normal, and not every child in my class at school was being used as a sex object by the adults around them. I became ashamed, and that shame strengthened my resolve to keep it secret.

3

'Where are you going?'

'Home,' I said. I had just walked into the entryway of the May Court block of flats, and the man who asked me the question was leaning against the concrete stairs, watching me. He was tall, well built, with dark curly hair, and he had a cigarette in his mouth. Nowadays, May Court has been renovated and upgraded, and there is an entry-phone system so that residents can vet who gets inside. Back then, the stairwells were open, with doorways on both sides. Some people used them as a cut through to get to other blocks of flats. They smelt of stale urine, there were empty beer cans and other litter lying around, and I hated lingering there.

I knew the man who asked me the question. Billy had given up his ice-cream van, and was now distributing catalogues and selling kitchen goods as a door-to-door salesman. Scooby, the man who had spoken to me, worked with him. I'd seen him at our flat when the deliveries of goods arrived to be distributed. I knew he lived nearby, in another block of flats.

I turned from him to walk up the stairs when he suddenly grabbed me from behind and pulled me to the back of the stairs. He yanked my black trousers down, forcing one leg free, and then lifted me and raped me. It was so sudden and brutal that I did not have time to cry out. It lasted a very short time, but it was a very public place and he risked being caught. I squeezed my eyes tight shut and let him do it: it was all I expected in life.

He put me down roughly and ordered me to put my trousers back on. As he fastened his own clothes he said, 'Don't go up to your flat right now, because that's where I'm going.'

I sat down on the hard concrete stairs and cried. I did not know then that Mum and Billy had told him he could rape me, sanctioning his attack on me. I assumed, because he told me to wait before going home, that they didn't know. I felt desperately miserable and unsafe: at least the other abuse had always been organised. Not a random assault in a public place. I was relieved that none of my friends had seen, but mortified at the thought that they so easily could have. Looking back, I can see his actions had probably been agreed in advance by Mum and Billy.

How do paedophiles recognise each other? How do they meet and share their warped appetites? Twenty years ago, when these things were happening to me, there was no

Internet highway to bring them together. Living around us in that tough district of Muirhouse there must have been hundreds of decent, normal men, with straightforward sexual desires. But somehow, in ways I don't understand, my mum attracted paedophiles into her orbit. She was a magnet for them: almost every man she ever became involved with was a paedophile. Billy, too: practically every man he ever brought back to our home turned out to be a paedophile. It couldn't just be coincidence, but I've never worked out how he recruited them.

When I finally went up to the flat, Scooby, whose real name is John O'Flaherty, was still there, talking to Mum and Billy. When he left, I told them what had happened. I was still very shaken by the suddenness and the brutality of the attack. I felt it was wrong that he had grabbed me. I was completely inured to the hell of sexual abuse, but the violent and public nature of it scared me in a way I wasn't used to. Perhaps, in a childish way, I also subconsciously felt that he was encroaching on their territory: they stage-managed my abuse, it didn't happen in dirty stairwells.

'I'll deal with it,' Billy said, after I told them.

The following day, when I walked in after school, Scooby was there, with Mum and Billy. I took one look around the living room and realised that they were all in this together. I was told to take my trousers off, and the abuse began, with all three of them taking part. This was Billy's way of 'dealing with it': he had brought the man who raped me into their sex games. Mum, as usual, was fully involved.

Afterwards they didn't even have to tell me to go away

and play. I knew the drill. I was always so glad when it was over, but I still had no concept of how wrong it was. I was seven years old by this time, and it had been my way of life for two years. Sex happened to me, and afterwards everyone behaved like normal, watching the telly, eating their tea, talking about ordinary everyday things.

From that day on, for the next couple of years, Scooby joined in with the abuse at our home. If I arrived home from school and he was there, I knew what was going to happen. I'd be told to go to the bedroom and take my clothes off. More often, though, I was told to go to Scooby's own flat, which was nearby. There, he got down to business straightaway. There were no preliminaries, he didn't talk to me apart from ordering me to take my trousers off. It was a dirty, smelly, dark flat, with plates of mouldy food, overflowing ashtrays, and piles of papers and clothes on the floor. Even at your lowest ebb, if you were homeless and cold and alone, you would not want to stay in that flat. He was as dirty as his home; he was smelly, greasy and he always wore the same stained, brown trousers.

I've realised, as I've tried to recall in recent years the details of my childhood, both to give evidence to the police and to write this book, that when I describe the men who abused me, it is their trousers that I remember, not their shirts or jackets or anything else they wore. My memories of them all are from the perspective of the abuse. That's all they ever were to me: men who gratified their sexual needs on my small body.

When he'd finished with me, Scooby would simply say,

'Go home.' I was never given presents, never rewarded in any way, never praised. I was, to him and the others, an object without feelings, thoughts, pain. Probably Billy had told Scooby: 'Don't worry about her, she knows to keep quiet. I've seen to it.'

Until I was seven the home of my other nana and granddad, my mum's parents, had always been a refuge for me. I used to love going to their house in Blackridge about half an hour's drive outside Edinburgh (their house has since been pulled down). Granddad used to spend a lot of time in the bedroom watching TV, and Heather and I used to scamper upstairs to sit with him. He had a tape player, and he used to let us choose tapes to play in it. He also had an assortment of old radios he was always tinkering with, which we were allowed to play with too. He didn't care if we broke them, he never shouted at us. Best of all, he used to let me play with his hair, combing it and putting bobbles into it, and he'd say, 'I'll buy you a hairdresser's when you're bigger.'

Sometimes he'd walk Heather and me 'doon the street' to the shop, and buy us sweets. As far as I was concerned, he was a really good granddad, particularly when my only comparison was Granddad King.

I used to lie on the bed next to Granddad watching TV, and I felt happy and secure there. I'd done it many times, and felt I could trust him and briefly feel safe. But it changed. Maybe I grew to the age that he liked little girls, I don't know. Even after all my experience, I don't understand how the urges of a paedophile work. All I know is that one day, as I lay next to him watching a film, he rolled on top of me, fully clothed, and started simulating sex with me. After a few seconds he rolled off, undid his zip, told me to pull my trousers down, and then had sex with me. He said nothing. I was, as usual, petrified and rigid, but I knew to stay silent.

When it was over he said, 'Don't tell your nan, or she'll go mad. Don't tell anyone or you'll be in serious trouble.'

Then he started watching the telly again. I suppose I should have been shocked, but I was being regularly abused at home by Mum, Billy and Scooby, and taken frequently to the House of Hell to be subjected to a far worse level of horrific abuse. Granddad was just another man doing it to me, and it was what I had come to expect from my life.

It did not even stop me going up to his room – I still wanted to play with his hair. Many times nothing abusive happened. He never did anything to me if Heather was there, and he never forced me to go upstairs. Sometimes he'd say, 'Do you want to come up and watch TV?' Sometimes I went, but sometimes I didn't, and he never ordered me to go up. And, even when we were watching TV, sometimes it happened, sometimes it didn't. Again, like Mum and Billy, it was confusing, because he was in other ways a perfect grandparent.

Soon after Granddad started abusing me, I became very ill. I was spending the school summer holidays staying with Mum's parents, Nana and Granddad, and I kept being sick. I was also drinking lots. Nana bought squash and cola by the crateful, and I was downing it faster than they could buy it. One day, when Mum came round to visit, they decided to call a doctor. In fact, I was taken to the doctors' surgery three or four times, but my parents were always told I had an infection. Eventually, when Mum noticed blood in my vomit, she and Billy and Auntie Brenda put me in the car and took me straight to hospital. I sat in the back with Auntie Brenda, and I remember being sick all over her as she cuddled me. It is almost the last thing I remember of that day. I have a vague recollection of getting to the hospital, and people gathered around me talking. But they all seemed very far away, and the sound of their voices became distant.

The next thing I recall is waking up, with Mum sitting next to my bed. I had no idea that it was ten days later, and I had been in a diabetic coma all that time. Apparently, Mum had been at the hospital the whole time, sleeping next to me. I'm sure the doctors and nurses thought she was a perfect, devoted mother. Billy, too, came every day to see me. Looking back, it was probably the longest period of my childhood without abuse. But because I'd been unwell and staying with Nana and Granddad I'd not been to the House of Hell for several days so it wasn't suprising no one noticed any injuries or anything that would have made them suspicious enough to ask questions.

I was diagnosed with Type One diabetes, which means I have to inject insulin daily. At first it was only twice a day, but now it's four times a day, and I will have to do it for the rest of my life. In my files at the diabetic clinic is a photograph of me at the time I was in the coma, lying in bed with two drips in me. I was so skinny you can see every bone of my ribcage.

By coincidence, as he wasn't a blood relative of mine, Billy was also diabetic, and I first understood what was wrong with me when I heard Mum telling someone, 'She's got what Billy's got.' I knew he had to inject insulin regularly, I'd seen his medication at our flat, although I don't remember actually seeing him do it. But I went into a blind panic when I heard her say it, because of the injections.

Like any small child, I hated needles and I used to scream when anyone approached me with one. Mum had to be taught how to do my injections. I can also remember being made to pedal fast on an exercise bike in the hospital to cause a diabetic hypo, which is what happens before you fall into a diabetic coma, caused by blood sugars falling too fast and too low. They made me do the test so that I would recognise what a diabetic hypo felt like and know what to do to stop myself from falling into a coma again. I can't remember how long they kept me in hospital, but as soon as my insulin levels were stabilised I went home.

I had a surprise visitor while I was in hospital: Tam, my father, turned up with his brother, Uncle Kenny. I hadn't seen him for a couple of years, and I don't remember seeing him again until I was grown up. He brought me a large panda bear toy, which I kept for years. I recognised him straightaway, but I think the days of wanting him to come home had long passed, and I didn't pin any hopes on seeing him again or having him back in my life. I don't know how he heard I was ill, I don't think Mum would have told him.

At first Mum did my injections for me, but by the time I was nine or ten I was doing them myself. Every school I went to had to be told about my diabetes, and a supply of Dextrosol tablets kept on hand in case my blood-sugar level fell. I always had to have them before P.E.

I know there are doctors and researchers who believe that stress can cause diabetes, or at least exacerbate it. Ten years after I was diagnosed, Heather was also found to be a Type One insulin-dependent diabetic. There can hardly have been two little girls more under stress than we were.

Over the next three years Granddad abused me about fifteen times – so you can see how, from my perspective, it was so much more acceptable than the abuse I received from the Kings, which was much more regular, horrifying and painful. Auntie Brenda was still living at home with Granddad and Nana when it started. She didn't know it was happening as she was going out to work every day. If she was at home, I loved most of all being with her, in her bedroom. That way it meant that Granddad didn't get too many chances to have sex with me either: perhaps if he had had more opportunities, he would have abused me more.

Did Nana know? I'm sure, looking back, she must have done. She never participated in it, but she turned a blind eye. I think, on reflection from my adult standpoint, that she would have had to be blind and dumb not to know that something was going on. As a child, though, I did what Granddad told me, and never said anything to anyone.

Many years later, when my mum was being investigated by the police over her abuse of me, I found out that she, too, had been abused by Granddad for years when she was a child. I assume Nana must have turned a blind eye to this, too. It would be hard not to know or suspect what was going on. Unlike Mum, who participated with Billy and his parents in their abuse of me, Nana played the more familiar role of women with abusive husbands: she silently condoned it by doing nothing to stop him. She, too, betrayed her daughter and me.

Billy and his parents hardly ever touched a drop of alcohol, but Granddad was a heavy drinker – although his abuse of me happened whether he was drunk or sober. He had been a coalman in his earlier life, but when I knew him he didn't work. I once saw him, when he was drunk, being violent towards Nana: he hit her over the head with an ashtray, splitting her head open. But, despite this, I was never frightened of him. They argued quite a lot, but I never paid any attention to it, and he was never violent or verbally abusive towards me.

I'm not offering this as an excuse, or in any way justifying what he did: all I know is that, against the scale of abuse that I was suffering on an almost daily basis, Granddad was not for me a big problem. Looking back, I realise that he actually played a key role in the horrors of my childhood, not just because of the abuse he inflicted. It was Granddad who introduced Mum to Billy, and it was from this meeting that all my problems flowed. I can trace all the blame back to him if I choose to, but what he did to me physically was nowhere near on the same scale as that carried out at the House of Hell.

When Auntie Brenda left home to set up her own life with my Uncle Bilko (his real name is William, but he's always called Bilko) and their daughter Leanne, the first of their three children, they moved into a house across the road from Nana and Granddad. I was ten at the time, and from that day onwards I never spent very much time in Nana and Granddad's house. The most I ever did was call in briefly, and then go across the road to Auntie Brenda's, where I really did finally have a haven.

Auntie Brenda was to prove to be a real heroine. She was someone who loved me, cared for me and made me feel safe, when just about every other adult in my life was abusing me. I loved staying at her house and playing with her babies – just as she had loved playing with me when I was born. She would brush my hair, let me experiment with her make-up or try on her shoes. It was she who took me to have my ears pierced. With her I could do all the normal things that little girls love. It was the only place where I could truly be a carefree child, and I used to beg to be allowed to go there. The happiest times of my childhood were the school holidays, when I would stay with Brenda and Bilko for at least a couple of weeks.

Not only was I happy to be with her, but I was also happy not to be Granddad's victim any more. Granddad never said anything about me not going there, and I was of course relieved to be away from the constant threat of one area of abuse I suffered. I never once thought about what was happening in Granddad's house without me there.

It honestly never occurred to me that he simply substituted Heather for me. Although I now know that he had molested her a few times, I think it was after I was no longer available that she came in for a lot more abuse, which lasted much longer and was much worse than anything he did to me. I think at the time all my childish responses were concentrated on my own survival, at any expense. And besides, even if I had known or suspected that Heather was being raped by him, what could I have done? It surprises me when I look back, but Heather and I never talked about the abuse when we were children. Even when we were abused together, by the Kings, it was never discussed between us. It was so impressed upon us that we must never mention it, never tell anyone, that we could not even comfort each other.

4

When I was nine, we moved away from Edinburgh, forty-five miles north to the pretty little village of Abernethy, near Perth. I don't know why we suddenly left Edinburgh, nobody ever explained the move to me. We moved all the time, constantly changing from flat to flat around Edinburgh. In retrospect, I wonder if it was because Mum and Billy never wanted to risk me becoming settled in one school for too long, in case I built up relationships with teachers and staff, and eventually had the confidence to speak out about what was happening.

Abernethy is a beautiful village and is used by tourists as a base for exploring Perthshire or for visiting the famous golf clubs of Carnoustie, Gleneagles and St Andrews, which are all on its doorstep. The village itself is small and steeped in history, and the school I attended there was tiny compared to the busy primary schools in Edinburgh. It was set in woodland, with more green space around it than I had ever seen in my life. I was so used to changing schools that it didn't seem strange once again being the new girl who knew nobody. I didn't even have Heather for company, as it was at Abernethy that she was first assessed as in need of special school education. I was briefly happy at the school, and I remember enjoying learning to play the recorder there.

Abernethy may be a lovely place, but we weren't really going up in the world; we moved into a mobile home on a caravan park. At first I was sad we had moved. I missed my friends and the vast countryside was overwhelming after the busy streets of Edinburgh, although I cannot remember ever being taken to explore it. All I remember is the caravan park, with its rows of mobile homes, and green spaces alongside the red-shale roadways where we could play safely. There was a field within the confines of the caravan park, which Heather and I used to explore. I have no memory of any other children living there, but I do remember a woman in a mobile home opposite who had two rabbits that I was allowed to hold and stroke. Because our mobile home was small Mum used to do the washing outside, in an old twin-tub washing machine. In bad weather it was hard to keep the place clean, as we trailed mud inside all the time. As a child I was terrified of mice, and there were little field mice living all around us. Things were certainly very different to life in Edinburgh.

The great compensation was that we were much further away from the House of Hell. We still got taken back to visit Granddad King's home, and the downside was that the journey, and its anticipatory fear, lasted much longer. But now we only visited once a week, which made a welcome reduction in the torture.

Abernethy was not a respite, however, because it was here that one of the most dramatically awful events of my childhood happened. One evening Mum had gone out and Heather and I had been told to go to bed early, instead of being allowed to stay up and play. Soon after we were in our bunk beds, Billy came in and tied a cloth across my face, blindfolding me. Nothing like this had ever happened before, and I had to hold back from crying even before anything happened. I knew that if I was taken from my bed that it would be bad, but I usually knew what it would entail. This was new, and I was gripped by fear. Billy led me by the hand to the other bedroom, and lay me down on my back on the bed. He took my nightie and pants off and I lay there naked and blindfolded. I did not dare cry, because that always made everything worse, but my breath came in gulping sobs as I fought to keep my panic at bay.

I could hear movement in the room and whispers. It was impossible to make out what the voices were saying, as they were trying to be quiet, but I obviously knew that Billy was not alone, which scared me. Much as I hated his abuse, I knew what it involved. This was new, and very frightening.

Then a man climbed on top of me and had sex with me. I could not see who it was, but I knew it was a big person. I also knew it wasn't Billy, as I would have recognised his grotesque tyres of fat, and I was very familiar with the feeling of his weight on top of me. When this man had finished with me a second man, much skinnier and smaller, had anal sex with me (this was happening to me regularly at the House of Hell as well so I knew what he was doing). Finally, a third man had sex with me. Again, I had no idea who it was, but I was certain it wasn't Billy. I could hear them all muttering to each other, but I still could not make out what they were saying. I was completely in the dark. It was much more terrifying than being abused with my eyes open: the fear of the unknown is the greatest fear of all. The whole event was so overwhelmingly horrifying that despite my best efforts, I cried out with pain, and I begged and begged for them to stop. Perhaps I hoped that, among the strangers, there would be one who would take pity on a naked, terrified nine-year-old girl. But, of course, it would have been a vain hope.

After they had all finished I was guided back to my own bed by Billy, and I can remember the feeling of relief when I realised I was back in my own room. He did not remove the blindfold until I was on my bed.

I lay still, sobbing silently: I was terrified of making a noise in case they came for me again, and I also didn't want to worry Heather, who was asleep above me in the top bunk. Most of all, I didn't want to give them the satisfaction of knowing I was crying. I could feel blood trickling between my legs, but I did not dare get out of bed to wash or to ask for help. Eventually, like so many nights before, I cried myself to sleep. The next day I was still in pain, which was unusual after so many years of abuse: as the abuse continued through my childhood, the physical pain of having sex, conventionally or anally, with large men, had receded. One pain that I often had afterwards was an excruciating nipping pain when I peed. I know now it was cystitis, but I was never given any treatment for it, and it happened frequently. It was the worst pain of all, taking my breath away, and lasting for days, a legacy that did not allow me to forget what had happened to me.

It wasn't until many years later that I discovered the identities of the men in that room. One of them was John O'Flaherty, alias Scooby. The other two I can't name, because they are the subject of ongoing police investigations. But the most horrific fact, which I didn't learn until years later, was that my mother was present throughout the entire gang rape. She watched and supervised, and she heard me crying out for help and for it all to end. Once again, she was guilty of the grossest neglect and abuse of one of her own little girls. Throughout the years, I had been sure she had gone out that night, with one of the men who, I later found out, was in fact part of the gang rape. She *did* go out, I can remember her going, but she must have returned after I'd been put to bed with Heather.

It was she herself who told me she had been there. When I heard, fifteen years later, I felt that deep sense of betrayal I had as a small child all over again. Why? I knew she was involved in so much, and she had been present at the worst of the orgies in the House of Hell, so why was I so hurt and angry that she had been there for this particularly horrible rape? I don't really know, but perhaps at some deeply subconscious level I still clung to the idea that she was my mum and so wouldn't stand by while something as dreadful as this happened to me. But she did.

Years later, when everything came out in court, John O'Flaherty made a full confession, and in it he said I was blindfolded and raped several times. He also said that Granddad took part in gang rapes of me when my eyes were covered. I only have memories of this one incident in the mobile home. Perhaps I have blocked the others out of my memory, but I don't think this is likely as I haven't blocked out of my memory the most horrific abuse of all, at the House of Hell.

More likely, I believe, is that other little girls were subjected to this treatment, that other children were blindfolded and raped by the same gang of paedophiles. He would not remember the difference: after all, to them we did not exist as human beings, vulnerable children with our own fears and hopes. We were simply pieces of meat, bodies to be treated as inanimate sex toys. One small frightened girl must be much like any other to these animals. No other victims have come forward. But, as you will see much later in this book, it takes a great deal of courage to step out of the shadows and confront your abusers. There are, I think, other children, now grown up, who were abused by the same men who destroyed my childhood. I feel deeply for them, as I know only too well how difficult it is to stand up and confront abusers, even years later. I also know that not everyone has the support I have had.

After a year we came back from Abernethy to Edinburgh, to Muirhouse Green, horribly close to the House of Hell: it took only two minutes to walk there. Again, no reason was given for the move: it just happened. A van was hired, our possessions loaded on, and we followed it in the car.

Once back in Edinburgh, Billy resumed his door-to-door sales round, but Scooby no longer worked with him. Another of his friends, Morris Petch, took over. I was about ten when this happened. Morris Petch was always known as Mo. He was tall, dark haired, skinny, scruffy and smelly and, like Scooby, he lived on his own in one of the blocks of flats near us. I first saw him at our place with Billy, but nothing happened while he was there. However, within a few days of him first coming on to the scene, Billy told me to go to Mo's flat. He didn't say why, but he didn't need to. For me, a man who did not abuse me was a rarity. I naturally assumed all men would have sex with me, and as far as Mo was concerned, I was right.

As soon as I got to his flat, which was in a block at a right angle to ours and no more than three minutes' walk away, he told me to take my trousers off and he raped me. His flat was very dark, because the curtains were always drawn, and it felt incredibly frightening to be there. He had painted one wall with scrolls, birds, love hearts and balloons, and there were names in fancy lettering everywhere, in lots of different colours. I suppose he was quite a good artist, but the effect was threatening and sinister. The only furniture that I remember was a bed settee, which was already opened up when I arrived, filling most of the small room. There were beer cans, plates with mouldy food strewn on the floor, and dirty cups everywhere. He was as smelly and dirty as his flat, just like Scooby.

The abuse followed the pattern I was accustomed to: he hardly spoke apart from giving me orders, and when it was over he said, 'You can go back now.' I went home, where Billy and Mum were, but they didn't speak to me about what had happened. Ten minutes later Mo actually turned up at our flat. As usual, everyone carried on as if nothing had happened; watching TV, chatting, Mum cooking a meal.

Sometimes Mo would come over to our house and have group sex with Mum and Billy, and I'd have to take part. He particularly seemed to like watching me do things to Mum. He abused me and Heather together, but not at our flat, it was always at his own. I didn't know until years later that Scooby also abused Heather, because, unlike Mo, he never did it to both of us at the same time. Looking back, it strikes me again how strange it is that we never talked about what was happening to us until years later. I think we were both so paralysed with fear that it was easier to say nothing and push it below the level of our everyday consciousness. That was the only way we could survive and, for Heather, who by nature lives very much in the present and doesn't spend time reflecting on the events of her life, it was possibly easier than it was for me.

Sometimes Mum would take me or send me to Mo's house and say, 'Don't tell your Dad.' Of course I didn't tell Billy, I didn't tell anyone. I was used to all my abusers, apart from Mum and Billy, telling me not to tell the others. I've never worked out why I was not supposed to tell him about Mo, as he knew about everything else that was going on. It certainly wasn't because she was getting any trade-off from Mo, such as money, because he had nothing. On other occasions I would bump into Mo in the street and he would say, 'Come up to my place in ten minutes.' I never dared to disobey.

He was so close to Billy and Mum that in 1991, when I was eleven, he spent Christmas with us. He was there on Christmas Eve and Christmas Day, and I was abused every day of that holiday.

Despite what was happening in our lives, Christmas was still an exciting time for Heather and me. About two or three weeks before, we would climb into the same bed and whisper together about how it would be on the big day. We would make plans, telling each other how early we would go to bed the night before, and how we would wake each other up in the morning. We would discuss at length whether we would open the biggest present first, or start with the smallest. It became our Christmas ritual, and even if we were living in a flat where we had separate bedrooms, for that couple of weeks we would always share. Every evening before bed Heather would whisper to me: 'Tell me about Christmas.'

It was one point of the year when we'd always feel slightly happier and could indulge in our little ritual. It was the only time when I willingly went to bed early. Most of the year I tried to put it off, vainly hoping to stave off the moment that Billy came into my room to take me for his sex games.

Every year, a couple of weeks before Christmas, we would help Mum and Billy put the decorations up. We'd make paper chains to hang across the ceilings, and we had a Christmas tree, with perfect, sparkling fairy lights. We would hang our stockings on the tree, as we didn't have a fireplace to hang them from. School would be full of Christmas as well, with decorations and nativity plays and carol concerts, and my excitement would mount as Christmas Day approached. I knew the abuse would still happen, but for one whole day I would be able to shut it out of my mind because I had something so much better to distract me.

On Christmas Day we would get up really early, and wake Mum and Billy, who would come with us to the living room. We were not allowed in there without them, but they never minded being dragged out of bed by two excited little girls. There would always be two big piles of parcels, and we'd rip them open happily, just as Heather and I had planned in our whispered bedtime ritual. We'd each get one expensive present and lots of little things, and there would be presents from Nana and Auntie Brenda as well.

Nobody in my family apart from me likes turkey, so Christmas dinner would be a regular roast, but we would have crackers and wear paper hats and read the jokes. Just like millions of other families up and down the country. There would be chocolate and sweets and nuts, and the television would be on with all the Christmas programmes.

As soon as we were old enough to have pocket money we bought presents for Mum. I would buy her silly little teddy bears with messages like 'I love you' and 'Huggy bear' on them. I was always very excited about buying presents for her, and watching her open them was almost as good as getting them myself. Once for her birthday we told Billy that we wanted to get her a 'MUM' ring, and he got it for us to give to her. She never showed any emotion when she got presents from us, never hugged us to show her appreciation, and I didn't realise until I was much older that it wasn't normal to show no emotion towards your own daughters.

Boxing Day was Billy's birthday, but I don't remember ever buying him a present. Mum would get something for him and put our name on it. We'd maybe go to see Nana and Granddad, or they would come to us. I'm happy to say the Kings never came to our house, and I don't remember ever being taken to them to be abused over Christmas. They must have had family around or known that the neighbours would be in.

But I was certainly abused at home. The year that Mo came to spend Christmas with us Heather and I went to bed early on Christmas Eve, filled with childish anticipation of the next morning. We could hear the sound of Christmas songs from the television in the living room, and at first we were too excited to sleep. I knew Mo was there, with Mum and Billy, and I knew it would only be a matter of time before I was told to go through to the other bedroom. Eventually we fell asleep, exhausted with excitement. Then, inevitably, it happened. Billy quietly knocked on the door and said, 'Come through here, Dana.'

Heather slept on, while I went through to the room where Mum was lying naked on the bed and Mo, trousers off, was waiting. As usual, Billy acted as a sort of ringmaster, telling me what to do to Mum's body. She lay there, letting it all happen, then watching as both the men raped me.

I have to ask the question again: How could she? She should have been cuddling me, telling me to go to sleep or Santa wouldn't come, happily planning the surprises she had for her little girls the next day. Instead, it was like any other night for them. I was their plaything and it didn't matter whether I had been good or bad that year.

The thrill of Christmas morning, however, was not dampened by the night-time activities: I was so used to Mum's and Billy's actions that they no longer affected me for long. Heather and I woke early, and there were the two eagerly anticipated piles of presents begging to be opened as quickly as possible. Heather's were stacked on the settee and mine on one of the chairs. We happily ripped off the gaudy wrapping paper to find new clothes, toys, chocolates. Then we took everything to our room, and dressed in our new clothes while Mum and Billy started preparing the Christmas lunch.

Later in the morning Mo reappeared, and my heart sank.

I had been hoping that this day would be easy, that I had done my penance with the previous night's orgy and deserved a break. I was so happy, playing with my new things and enjoying the warm smell of the food being cooked, but now his presence overshadowed all of that.

We had a lovely meal, roast chicken with all the trimmings followed by ice cream and jelly trifles. We pulled crackers and laughed at the stupid jokes, and I managed to enjoy myself even though, across the table from me, looking ridiculous in a paper hat and joining in like he was part of the family, was the repulsive man I knew would rape me before the end of the day. After lunch we watched television and ate chocolates, but the edge had gone from my pleasure because I dreaded what was to come. After the meal Mo said he was going home. I briefly hoped I had escaped but soon realised with dread that I would most likely be sent over to his place instead, which always made it so much worse.

True enough, after a little while I was called through to the kitchen where Billy was doing the dishes with Mum, and he told me to go over to Mo's. I didn't outwardly rebel or object, I always did what I was told, but before I went I slipped into my bedroom and changed out of my brand-new Christmas clothes, and into some old trousers and a top. I wanted to keep my new clothes special and not spoil them by wearing them in that disgusting flat.

Outside was deserted because it was Christmas afternoon and I didn't see another person. Through every window that I passed I could see the flickering of fairy lights and the bright television screens, and I knew that families were relaxing after stuffing themselves with food, enjoying peaceful afternoons watching the children play with their new toys. I wanted so much to be part of that normal world.

At Mo's I was forced to have oral sex with him, which made me feel like I might throw up my Christmas lunch. Then he raped me. I ran back home as fast as I could, back to Christmas and my new things, pushing all thoughts of the abuse out of my head. That night, Billy also raped me. Boxing Day, too, ended with the nightly ritual of abuse. Yet, whatever they did, they never managed to extinguish the spirit of Christmas in me. It is still, for me, the best time of the year, and I always feel a tingle of anticipation when the Christmas lights go on and the shop window displays are magically lit up and everywhere the air is filled with Christmas music.

It was soon after we got back from Abernethy that Billy and Mum were married. It took place in a Register Office, with Billy's sister as a witness, and a man who was lodging with us at the time standing in as Billy's best man. I don't remember much about it, except that Heather and I had to wear pink dresses. They were so girlie that even I thought they were stupid. Mum wore a cream suit. The reception was at the House of Hell, where food and drink was laid on: imagine the irony of everyone toasting the 'happy couple' in the place where they took part in such appalling cruelty.

I was still being ordered to go to the House of Hell regularly, as well as being abused by Mo and being removed from my bed in the night by Billy, encouraged and helped by my mother in his abuse. Of course, I frequently fantasised about running away, but I was too scared. Where would I go? I was too ashamed to tell anyone about the abuse, even Auntie Brenda. Who would believe me? It would be my word against Mum and Billy, and to the world outside our four walls they continued to appear to be good parents. Heather wouldn't be able to back me up, as she was never abused by them: to this day she thinks Billy was an angel, even though he was the one who sent her to the House of Hell, and to be abused by Scooby and Mo. I still struggle to understand why this is, though for her he really was like a father, generous and kind in so many ways. Heather still loves Mum, too; although, like me, she has some mixed emotions.

In a childish, unrealised sort of way, I often thought about death. I was scared of it, but at the same time it clearly offered an escape. If I died I could not be abused any more; there would be no more pain. I did make one attempt to kill myself when I was ten. But it was done out of opportunity and not thought through, so I didn't come close to succeeding. I found a jagged piece of glass in the park and dragged it right down my arm. I didn't think it had gone deep enough to draw blood, but at some point it must have hit a vein, because suddenly blood was gushing out. I was terrified, and held my jumper against it tight until it stopped bleeding. I didn't tell Mum, and she never commented on my bloodstained jumper. Another time, I thought about climbing on to the roof of the school and throwing myself off. I'd seen other kids get up there, but when I tried I was too small to reach the roof and too scared to go through with it anyway.

I had no sense of what death would mean. I had no real concept of religion, of there being an afterlife: the promise of Heaven or the threat of Hell. There was no religion at home, and although I had briefly attended a Church school, where we said prayers, I was never given the psychological lifeboat of a faith to help me through the darkest times. When I prayed for the abuse to stop I had no idea to whom I was praying. I simply wanted some external force to intervene on my behalf.

Eventually it did: things were changing at the House of Hell. Nana King developed dementia. I suppose I should have felt sorry for this small, confused woman wandering aimlessly around her own home, lost in the fug of her receding memory, but she had been so evil towards me and Heather that I felt no pity for her. Besides, she still took part in the abuse. She never spoke, but she'd do all the things they wanted her to do during their orgies. Eventually, she became so confused that her husband needed help looking after her. But it didn't stop the abuse.

To my great delight, in February 1992, when I was twelve, Granddad King died. That was a good day for me, in fact I think of it as one of the best days of my entire life. He had a sudden heart attack at the bottom of the stairs in the House of Hell. Only three or four days earlier he had been abusing me while Nana King was in hospital for respite care. Mum and Billy were very upset about his death, but for me it was like being reborn. I couldn't show my feelings to them, but inside I was celebrating. My main tormentor, the most evil man I have ever encountered – and that's saying something – was dead. I knew the abuse would go on, because Billy would see to that, but, with Nana King also incapacitated, I was certain that the sadistic violence would be over. I spent a lot of time in my room over the next few days, because I could not let my relief show. When I was with Mum and Billy I made a point of looking sad on the outside, to match their mood, but inside I was rejoicing.

I couldn't share my joy with anybody outside the family, either, because I could never admit to what had been happening. But I remember waking up each morning and wondering for a few seconds why life felt good, then remembering he was dead, and celebrating silently all over again. With his death, Nana King moved to live with one of their daughters and I never saw her again. She died almost exactly two years later, and she was buried in the same grave as her husband. The inscription on the white marble headstone reads: *In loving memory of Peter King, died 1.2.1992. A dear husband, dad and granddad. Also his beloved wife Mary Walker, died 8.2.1994. A much-loved Mum and Nana.*

Even in death, they managed to behave as though everything in their family was normal. Nobody would ever guess from that pious memorial that in that grave lies two people who rivalled each other in sadistic cruelty and perversion. I didn't go to either of their funerals, but on the day each was put into the ground I celebrated in my heart.

* * *

By the time I was twelve the abuse from Mo had become relentless. We had moved again and for a while I was even made to stay with him overnight. I had no choice but to lie awake beside him in his stinking bed. It was terrifying and he would always rape me repeatedly. Those nights felt like they would never end. Eventually he moved flat too, in order to live closer to us. While I no longer had to stay overnight with him, the abuse continued for several more months. Then, as quickly as he first arrived in my life, he left. I don't know why, however, it was only a matter of a few months before another abuser came into my life. He was not part of the circle of paedophiles who surrounded my parents; he was an independent and solitary predator, although he knew my family well enough. He was also very different from any of the men who had abused me up to then: to all intents and purposes, he courted me. He would tell me that he loved me, he paid me compliments, made arrangements to meet me almost like a date, bought me cigarettes like I was a grown-up. It was, in many ways, more like an affair than an abusive relationship – except for the glaring and inexcusable fact that I was a child and he was a grown man, many years older than me.

I can't talk in any detail about him, because he is another of the men the police are continuing to investigate. But from the very beginning it was different. I am not in any way condoning his behaviour, other than to say he was not aggressive, he was not physically cruel, and he talked to me. That's more than any of the others did. To them I was an object, I had no choice; they didn't even see me as a human being. He made me feel special, he didn't have to force me; I went willingly. He'd tell me that he couldn't wait to see me, and for me it was so unusual to be valued by anyone, anyone at all, that I was bowled over by it.

Obviously, I now know that a twelve-year-old can't, and shouldn't have to, make adult decisions. In some ways I was very old for my years: I had seen and done far more than the average girl of my age. But I was physically immature: small and flat-chested. There cannot have been any doubt in his mind that I was a child, and this was reinforced by him telling me not to let anyone know what he was doing to me. He was well aware that it was wrong.

Mum and Billy knew all about his sexual relationship with me – I'm sure he also knew that Billy had abused me. After a while he would come to our home and conduct the relationship there, in front of them. They even made a video of him with me on his lap, when I was aged about thirteen. On the film he says 'Smile if you had sex last night', and he said it knowing full well that he and I had. I didn't love him, but I liked him and looked forward to seeing him. I did not enjoy the sex, but I had no notion that sex was supposed to be enjoyable, and he did not deliberately hurt me.

Although, like most abused children, I was to some extent kept isolated from other families – mainly because we were constantly on the move – I did have some friends outside my own family. When I started at Craigroyston High School, aged twelve, I became best friends with another girl called Michelle. Michelle Douglas and I only really hung around together at school, rarely seeing each other outside school.

For some years I had another friend I played with outside school, the best childhood friend I had. Her name was Catherine and her family lived close to us for a short while. I loved Catherine and her family. She was a few months older than me, which pushed her into a school year above me, but we were inseparable out of school. She had a dog we used to take for walks together. She was more daring than I was, and would climb on to the school roof while I hung around below keeping watch. We smoked our first cigarettes together, in the park up the road from home. We would both get pocket money – Billy would give me £2.50 – and we'd go halves on a packet of cigarettes.

Once, when Billy caught me smoking, he really told me off. He took the cigarette off me, squashed it into the ground with his foot, and said, 'You'd better not let me catch you smoking again. You're grounded.' I wasn't allowed out for a week.

Again, he was acting like a normal, loving parent who was concerned for his stepdaughter's health. He was right to try to stop me smoking – it's what any good parent would do – but, on the other hand, what he was doing to me in private, and letting other people do, not one of them ever using a condom, was infinitely more damaging than a few cigarettes. Mum actually encouraged me to smoke. From the age of about fourteen she gave me full packets of cigarettes every now and again. I guess she thought it made me more grown up, or she was using the cigarettes to bribe me to keep quiet about the abuse, although she never said so.

Catherine's mum was so lovely that I used to wish she was my mum. Sometimes when I was there Catherine would argue with her about things like doing the dishes or tidying up, just being a normal difficult adolescent, I suppose. But I would be thinking, *Why are you arguing about something so small? Your mum really loves you and looks after you.*

I could never tell Catherine these thoughts, because I could never admit to the fact that I was not loved at home. But I used to wish with all my heart that her life was my life.

Her dad was wonderful, too. He used to fool around with us, play-fighting and joining in with our silly games. I dreamed of having a family like that. I can remember one of Catherine's birthdays when her mum took us ten-pin bowling, and sometimes she would drive us to Lasswade stables for horse-riding lessons, which she paid for. Catherine's gran took us to the cinema once, to see *Hocus Pocus*. Catherine had a little sister, but she was thirteen years younger, so for many years Catherine had been an only child. We spent lots of time together, playing Peter Andre and Take That records, trying out make-up and doing each other's hair. They were the happiest times of my childhood, rivalled only by my visits to Auntie Brenda's.

Catherine had no clue about the secrets of my childhood. I used to sleep over at her home as often as I could. Billy and Mum used to say, 'Why do you want to stay there? It's only downstairs, you can see each other in the morning.' But they never stopped me from sleeping there. Catherine used to occasionally stay over at our flat, and Mum and Billy were very good at putting on the act of doting parents while she was there. I felt safe when she stayed, because I knew they wouldn't touch me with someone else there. They were always careful not to give anything away to strangers; they kept the abuse within a tight group of people who they knew had the same tastes as they had. They would never have risked abusing me while Catherine was there, and they would never have touched her. I believe there were other children being abused by the men who abused me, but I don't think they were random victims: I think they were most likely introduced in similar ways that we were. Even though Catherine was my closest friend, I couldn't tell her. As I grew older I became more and more ashamed about the abuse and I would have rather died than let anybody know. As a small child I had accepted it as normal, and I had been frightened into silence. Now I was a teenager, I understood how wrong it was, but I could not escape it, so my attitude was, *Whatever happens, happens. Just get on with it and get it over quickly.*

At high school I became more conscious of the fact that we were a poor family, in monetary terms. Nobody in that area was exactly loaded, but I began to realise that many of the others had better trainers and more clothes than I had. Not that I ever went without, and if I particularly asked for something, usually Mum and Billy would get it for me. Catherine always had nice clothes and more money than I had, but I didn't feel resentful. I never envied her, or anyone else, their money or possessions:

all I envied was the warmth and security of their normal, loving families.

When we moved to Ferry Road, yet another stop on our tour around the council flats of Edinburgh, I was not physically as close to Catherine, but we stayed best friends. I remember one Christmas she used some of her Christmas money to buy a 'Forever Friends' chain, which split in two so that she had half and I had half. I used to go to all her family parties, and I basked in the glow of feeling part of her loving, normal family life.

Our move to Ferry Road was to a ground-floor flat, which we needed because Billy was beginning to become quite ill, and frequently had to go into hospital. It was all to do with his diabetes. Mum would take me and Heather to visit him in hospital, and secretly I was always really pleased and relieved that he was there, because it meant that he couldn't abuse me. Even when he was home again, the abuse became less frequent because he was so often unwell. It never completely stopped, though, and I always had that feeling of dread in the pit of my stomach when I went to bed, hoping it would not be that night.

Catherine and Michelle didn't like each other, and they used to compete to be my best friend at school. One day they even had a fight over me. I tried to stay friends with both of them, but eventually Michelle and I drifted apart. I had other friends at school so it didn't bother me too much: I wouldn't say I was one of the most popular girls, but I was never unpopular or bullied. In fact, I loved school. It was a safe place, where nobody knew about my home life. I was the reverse of most kids: I loved walking through the gates first thing in the morning, and I hated it when lessons were over and we all headed for home, where life was anything but predictable.

Unlike my earlier school years, my time at Craigroyston was stable and secure: I actually stayed in the same school for four whole years. Perhaps Billy was just too ill to bother moving me around, or maybe he had simply stopped worrying about me telling anybody: as time went on, I suspect he felt more and more secure that the message to keep my mouth shut about the abuse had been well and truly absorbed by me. Heather, too, went to the same school for years, a school for children with learning difficulties (incidentally, the same one that Mum had attended).

So my time at Craigroyston was very happy and settled. I remember one teacher I really liked, Mr Flint. He was one of the few decent male role models in my life. I was older when I met him, and I knew by then that not all men were like the ones I met at home, and that only made me even more determined to keep the truth about my home life to myself. I knew it was shameful, dirty and at all costs to be kept secret. I felt that if anyone ever found out they would blame me, think I was part of it; I would be contaminated and nobody would want anything to do with me. I started to develop an act that I would perfect over the years: the act of pretending that I came from a good, loving family.

Mr Flint taught chemistry, and I chose it as one of my exam options just to be in his class. He organised skiing lessons at a dry ski slope, and then took a group of us skiing at Glenshee a couple of times. We'd leave at 6 a.m. in a minibus, and we'd get home very late after a full day skiing on real snow. I loved it. The night before I would always stay with Catherine, and her mum would get up at the crack of dawn to take us to the school to catch the minibus. Billy and Mum always gave me the money to go.

Mr Flint would drive the minibus, and at least one other teacher would be there with him. The money we paid for the trip included lunch, which we would have at a café. I loved those days: just the feeling of being out in the open air all day having the most fun with my friend Catherine.

Mum also bought me a guitar so I could take guitar lessons at school. They were generous like that, Mum and Billy. They certainly knew how to confuse a child's brain: if they had been horrible all the time, like Granddad and Nana King, it would have been easy to hate them. Just as I had enjoyed learning to play the recorder at primary school, I loved my high-school music lessons: my teacher, Kate Wiley, was my favourite. She was very down to earth and encouraging. The guitar teacher came into the school once a week, and I practised at home as much as I could and became quite good.

In my first year at Craigroyston our class went on a school camp, to a place not very far from Edinburgh, in the countryside. We went for five days, and three teachers came with us: Mrs Leckie, Mr Ward and Mr Flint. We slept in a hostel, four of us to a room. I was with Michelle (this was before we drifted apart) and two other girls, and on the first night we were so excited we giggled and talked and made each other laugh for hours. In the end Mrs Leckie came and sat in our room, to make us calm down and go to sleep.

I remember that camp as a magical time. We went to the cinema, we went on long walks and, in the evening, Mr Ward would play his guitar and we'd all sing along. Best of all, I could sleep undisturbed in my bed every night, knowing that nobody would come knocking at my door for sex. For one blissful week I felt normal, just like the other girls.

I enjoyed every bit of school. Although I didn't much like French, the teacher, Mrs Creighton, was really lovely, so I always tried my best for her. When we were asked to volunteer for the school choir, everyone pretended they only did it so they could get out of lessons. It wasn't cool to say you loved it. But secretly I did.

We had concerts twice a year where we sang, and sometimes I played the guitar. I remember Mum would come to them, usually bringing Heather with her. As always she played the doting mother well.

I loved our cookery classes, too. We paid a little bit of money each week for ingredients, and we could take home the things we made. Billy would usually enthusiastically eat my efforts. I also enjoyed Craft Design Technology, where I made a spatula and a keyring. Although Billy didn't come to the parents' evenings or concerts, if I got stuck on my maths or science homework, he would try to help: I couldn't ask Mum for help because of her learning difficulties.

When I was at primary school, I don't remember school being such a relief for me. I think it was because I went to so many different schools, and never felt entirely settled. With the added abuse of the House of Hell, I think it was hard to ever switch off from it all completely and to feel safe, no matter where I was. But Craigroyston High was a wonderful relief from the rest of my life, and I was really grateful for my time there. Even my favourite television programme, *Saved by the Bell*, was about life in a high school.

Billy's favourite programmes were *Star Trek* and *Prisoner Cell Block H*, and Mum always watched *EastEnders*. The TV was always on and a lot of the time they took no notice of it, but they always sat down to watch these.

When I was thirteen my periods started, and Mum and Billy told me that I would have to go on the Pill. Mum took me to the doctor. I don't know what she told him, but he was probably happy to prescribe contraceptives for any girl living in an area where so many girls had babies before they were school-leaving age. She certainly didn't tell him the real reason, which was that she and Billy were worried that I would get pregnant by my own step-father.

Neither of them had given me any sex education in the traditional, loving parental sense. But we had lessons at school. I found it embarrassing, sitting in a classroom full of giggling kids, all nudging each other about things which I had been experiencing from the age of five.

My past meant that I could never be like the other kids of my age, beginning to explore their own sexuality with each other. When I was thirteen, I did briefly have a boyfriend of my own age at school, but it didn't last very long. My friend asked me if I would go out with him, because he fancied me. I think we held hands and kissed a couple of times – it was all very innocent but, as with all adolescent crushes, it quickly fizzled out.

At this time I was seeing my 'boyfriend abuser', the man who made me feel special. I even told some of my friends at the time, and one of them met him. They seemed impressed, afterall he was tall, dark haired, well dressed, and he had a good job and a nice car. Compared to the likes of Billy, Scooby and Mo, he was very presentable and, more importantly, he told me he loved me, and those were words I never heard.

5

As I watched the coffin containing the mortal remains of Billy King being lowered into the same grave as his mother and father in Easter Road Cemetery, I felt an enormous sense of relief. He was dead; the third member of the evil King family had died peacefully in his sleep before justice could catch up with him, just as his mother and father had done.

I was fifteen when he died, and I was happy to take part in the public grieving at his funeral. It suited my pretence that we were a perfect little family and he had been a good, caring and much-loved stepdad. Now I could play the part even more convincingly, as he was out of the way and could never do or say anything to contradict the myth I was creating.

His death was very liberating for me, but unexpected. There was a knock on the door of our ground-floor flat, now in West Pilton Avenue, at about ten o'clock on the

Sunday morning that he died. Nobody was up, but I got out of bed to answer it. Auntie Brenda and Uncle Bilko were at the door with their three girls, Leanne, Zoe and Kayleigh – apparently Mum had agreed to look after the girls for the morning while they went to Ingatestone Market.

I went into the front bedroom to wake Mum and Billy. Billy, who was fifty-five years old, had come home from hospital a few days earlier, having discharged himself. I don't remember why he had been in hospital: I think probably his diabetes was out of control. He was very fat, weighing well over twenty stone, so it was inevitable that he'd get ill. Since he came home he had not left the flat, and had just moved between his bed and the chair in front of the telly.

'Mum, Brenda's here,' I called. There was no reply so I went out of the bedroom and said, 'I can't get them awake.'

Uncle Bilko followed me back into the room and shook Billy, but he still didn't move.

'I think he's dead,' he said. Mum by this time had woken up and was sitting up. When she heard these words she jumped out of bed. One of Billy's legs, covered in big, weeping ulcers, was dangling over the edge of the bed, and Bilko gave it a gentle kick. There was no response. I noticed a small trickle of blood coming from the corner of Billy's mouth.

After that, all I remember is the great commotion: an ambulance arrived, followed by a doctor then, finally, the body was taken away.

My feelings that day were very mixed. All around me, people were very upset. Mum was crying, Brenda and Bilko – who had no reason to suspect he was anything other than a good stepfather to me and Heather – were upset. I, too, was upset at first, and I rang my friend Louise and she came round to comfort me. Heather had been genuinely fond of him, or perhaps she simply felt secure with him because he had been around for so many years. Whatever the reason, she was deeply affected by his death, and very tearful. We were also, all of us, in shock. Although he had been ill, we had no idea that he was at death's door. His death certificate cited heart failure and 'complications arising from diabetes' among the causes of his death.

Billy's was the first funeral I ever attended. It started with a church service because, unbelievably, Billy claimed to be a Christian. Then we moved on to the cemetery in Easter Road, to the same plot where his parents were buried. There were lots of wreaths and one, in the shape of a heart, had the word 'Dad' written in flowers. Later, Mum paid for a small stone memorial, in the shape of an open book with a rose across it, and inscribed with the words, *In loving memory of a dear husband and dad, William King, died 3 December 1995.* It was laid in front of the much bigger monument to his parents.

I cried as the coffin was lowered, largely from relief, but tempered with a genuine feeling of loss. My emotions were, as so often, mixed. Billy left a big hole in all our lives. His funeral was well attended. Brenda and Bilko were crying – to them he was a wonderful man. Afterwards all the other mourners went to a pub to hold a wake for the kind, generous and well-liked man whom they had just buried, but for me that would have been one hypocrisy too many: I went home. I went to the bedroom he had shared with Mum and sat on the bed, where I had been raped so many times, and thought, *My God, it's over.*

At the service the priest had said that his spirit was now free, but so was mine. Part of me was ecstatic. I knew I would never again be woken in the night. He was at the heart of my problems, he was the one who made things happen. He had introduced me to all the other abusers, and although he himself was not the worst of them, he orchestrated all of it. Mum had been just as involved, but he was the organiser.

I remember thinking, *This is the start of my life. Where will it go from here?*

It was now just me, Mum and Heather, and I felt we could finally be a family, finally be happy. His death resulted in a real lightening of my spirit. I knew that Mum would never abuse me on her own. Besides, I was fifteen now, and able to stand up for myself. I'd been afraid of Billy; I was not afraid of Mum. I knew I was old enough to make decisions: nobody would ever again make me feel like a frightened little girl, nobody would make me do anything I did not want to do.

I felt a surge of elation; I felt the world was mine. 'I can do anything I want to do,' I said out loud to the empty flat.

Billy's death was three weeks before Christmas, which we spent with Brenda and Bilko. It was a difficult time; they were all still very emotional about the loss of Billy, whereas I was still buzzing from not being woken up in the night. Mum's grief did not last too long. She had never been much of a drinker, but after Billy's death she began to hit the bottle. She was going out most nights, and she'd leave me to look after Heather. Although Heather was fourteen, she wasn't mentally old enough to take care of herself or be left on her own. To bribe me to stay in with her, Mum would buy me large bottles of vodka. She'd hand them to me and say, 'Enjoy!' before she went off out. We never knew when she would be back. So for a brief time in my life I, too, drank a lot. For about a month, I was downing a bottle of vodka every evening. I did not really like it, and although I still have a drink now and again, I know that it's not an answer to anything. When I stopped having the vodka, I never missed it.

Much as I love Heather, I hated being left to look after her. I was young; I wanted my own life. I remember once exploding at Mum, 'You're drinking all the time, and you've got me and Heather to take care of. I can't do it.'

I think she often forgot that she had us. For all his many, many faults, Billy had provided her with a framework for her life, and while he was there she had been able to run a fairly normal home. Without him she left everything to me to do. Even my fear of him had been, in a strange way, a security. Now, while Mum was out gallivanting, there was nobody to tell me what to do, and that made me feel insecure.

I felt very disappointed. I had had really high hopes that with Billy out of the way she would become the mother I had always wanted, the mother she should have been. But her life was so erratic that for a time Heather lived with Nana and Granddad, who had moved back to Edinburgh and now lived about a five-minute walk away from us. Although I had no idea at the time, the horrors in Heather's life were escalating: the deaths of Billy, Granddad and Nana King did not bring her the same reprieve they brought me. She would have to wait a few more years for her life to be stable and happy.

Soon after Billy's death I noticed a small spot on my left leg, a red patch with a blister at the centre. Over the next few weeks it grew in size but I didn't think about it much until one day I banged my leg, and it erupted with pus. I still took very little notice, just sticking a plaster over it. But it grew and grew, and it began to look as if someone had taken a chunk out of my leg. I went to our GP, and was sent to hospital to see a dermatologist. Different creams were applied but nothing seemed to make any difference. I had to go to hospital every two days to have it dressed, but nobody seemed to know what it was or what to do about it. It grew to a long lesion down the lower half of my leg. It was not painful, but nothing seemed to halt its progress, and for the next couple of years my life was punctuated by trips to have it dressed every two days. It would be some time before anybody told me exactly what it was. My life was so busy that I didn't worry about it: it was an inconvenience more than anything else.

Billy's death happened in my last year at school, and I think the work I had to do for my exams kept my mind off the rest of my life. Because of his death, all my friends at school were feeling sorry for me and being very kind. My English teacher, Mrs Hubbard, had lost her own father not long before, and she talked to me about it. It was considerate of her, but the gulf between her genuine loss and my relief was huge. I can remember different people telling me that I would be all right. Outwardly, I faked being upset, but inside I felt, for the first time in my life, that I really would be all right. I was now in charge of my own destiny.

I stayed on at school until I had finished my exams, which were just before my sixteenth birthday. In Scotland we take similar exams to GCSEs, called Standard Grades. Despite everything that had happened in my life, I got good results: I passed English, maths, music, geography and French, as well as some cookery modules. I had to learn four guitar tunes for my music exam.

I didn't want to stay at school to get any more qualifications: I was desperate to leave home and get on with my own life. I wanted to escape my background, start afresh, do something just for me. Mum was drinking heavily, bringing men back, leaving me to look after

Heather all the time: I desperately needed a break. I was rowing with her a great deal. While Billy was alive I wouldn't have dared answer her back, but after his death I began to speak up for myself. Looking back, I can see that underneath the surface there were some huge issues between us, at least on my part. We were scratching at each other about relatively unimportant things because neither of us wanted the big confrontation. I should have said to her: 'Mum, how could you? How could you spend years so obsessed with a man that you willingly took part in his terrible abuse of your own daughter?'

But the words remained unspoken and, instead, we rowed about me having to babysit, me having to do so much around the house. I certainly didn't want to confront her: I saw Billy's death as a chance to put everything behind me, to pretend it had never happened, to pick up my life as if I was a normal teenage girl with nothing more dreadful in my past than the early death of my good and loving stepfather.

The push I needed to make me leave home was the arrival on the scene of Robert Heath, known as Rab. He and Mum took up together, and she wanted to move in with him. I did not like him: I was suspicious of all men who associated with Mum. It turns out that I had good cause to be, as Rab Heath later went to prison for sexually assaulting a girl I once knew in my nomadic childhood. We had lived near her family, and she and I used to play together. We didn't share it at the time, but we were both being sexually abused.

I left home and moved in with Brenda and Bilko and their daughters, in Pennywell. It was good to find myself in a normal family home, where people loved and cared about each other, and where life was organised around ordinary things, like Brenda's and Bilko's jobs and the children's school timetables. I shared a room with the children: Leanne, who was six at the time, Zoe, who was four, and baby Kayleigh. I helped out by looking after the children, but Brenda and Bilko were really good to me, letting me stay there free.

I applied to the council for my own council flat as soon as I moved in with Brenda and Bilko, and in a matter of a few months I was offered one. Council waiting lists can be very long, with people waiting years for a property, and Edinburgh is no exception. But if you are prepared to live in one of the rough areas of the city, you can be housed quickly. At least, I was. I was given a two-bedroomed flat in Royston Mains, a tough area where I felt frightened walking down the streets at night. I had all Mum's furniture and pots and pans, because she was moving in with Rab, taking Heather with her. There was enough basic stuff for me to live quite comfortably, although I could only afford carpet for the living room, and until I found a job, I had to live on benefits.

I was still close to Mum, and I saw her and Heather frequently. Brenda and Mum were also pretty close, although obviously Brenda had no idea about Mum's darker side. I think Brenda and I were both worried about her drinking too much, but we never discussed it.

When I finished school, I wanted to be a nurse at first, but then I decided I'd like to work as a childminder, because I really loved looking after Auntie Brenda's children. So I enrolled for a college course in the centre of Edinburgh.

Unfortunately, I didn't enjoy the childminding course, and only went for a couple of weeks. Although I had enjoyed school, I suddenly found that I didn't want to go back to sitting in a classroom filling in worksheets. I wanted to get on with the actual job of looking after children.

My best friend Catherine told me there was a job going where she worked, in the laundry of the Western General Hospital. It was boring because we spent most of our days there, folding towels and pressing blankets, but it was a job and a wage. I still found it very hard to manage the bills on my own, though. Catherine's mother was, as ever, very kind, giving me power cards to fund my electricity. Catherine was still living at home with her mum and dad, but she spent a lot of time at my flat.

I was determined to make a go of my independence, and one of the things I was most adamant about was that I would never take drugs. So many kids I knew had become caught up with drugs and I had seen how it had ruined their lives. I vowed I would not be joining them. And, after my mum pushed all that vodka on to me, I knew drink wasn't for me, either.

So many people who are abused as children turn to drugs, alcohol, self-harm or prostitution when they are older, or even become abusers themselves, perpetuating the misery that was once inflicted on them. I can't say where my self-preservation and inner strength came from, but I had the sense to know, even at sixteen, that I didn't want to go down any of those routes. I had seen how good life with a normal family could be – Catherine's, Auntie Brenda's – and that was what I longed for; I wasn't going to let anything jeopardise that dream. I'd known from the time I was very young that I wanted my own children, and I also knew that I'd do anything to make sure their young lives would be the complete opposite of mine.

I had grown up a lot faster than I should have done. Just as I never had a childhood, I also never had a normal adolescence. I never went out drinking with a crowd of girlfriends, picking up lads and having a laugh. I was scared to get drunk, very wary of people, unwilling to trust anyone I didn't know really well. My experiences in life had taught me that even those who seemed pleasant and plausible were often untrustworthy and out to take advantage of me. Yes, I wanted my own family, but I was determined I would always keep my independence.

As soon as I was seventeen I started having driving lessons, and I passed my test on my first attempt. None of the women in my family drove. The only people I knew who could drive were Billy and Uncle Bilko, and for most girls of my age and background, living in our area, the only four wheels they would ever own were on their babies' pushchairs. But for me, it seemed a much better idea to spend money on driving lessons than on clothes and make-up.

* * *

I may not have liked Mum's new partner Rab Heath, but I have one reason to be very grateful to him. It was through him that I met the man who was going to help me turn my life around, and who has been by my side ever since, helping me to confront my past and recover from my childhood years. Paul Kernachan lived across the road from Rab, but it was at the beach at Silverknowes when I was with Mum and Rab that I first met him. We had bumped into Paul who was with his partner and two children, and he and Rab chatted. I took very little notice of him on that occasion and could never have imagined the impact he'd one day have on my life.

Paul is twelve years older than me, and he was going through a very difficult time when I met him next, at Rab's house, where Mum and Heather were also living. His partner had left him twelve weeks earlier, and he was living on his own looking after his seven-year-old son, 'Young Paul'. He has another son, Ryan, who was only three months old at the time, and who was living with his ex-partner. Within three months Ryan also came to live with Paul, so he had two boys to look after, one of them a six-month-old baby.

Mum was hitting the bottle quite hard and, even though I was no longer living at home, she still expected me to be on hand to look after Heather. One night Paul came across to Rab's house and walked into the kitchen just as Mum and I were having a flaming row. In temper and frustration, I swept a milk bottle off the worktop at the very moment he walked through the door, so his first proper introduction to me was to be hit by a flying bottle of milk.

Initially, I didn't like him – I was too suspicious of men to allow myself to like any of them easily. But there were a few of us at the house that evening, messing around with a karaoke machine. At one stage Paul and I sang 'Up Where We Belong', the Buffy Sainte-Marie song. Then, somehow, we got talking – and we've never stopped talking to one another since. We made a connection which has survived, despite everything. We spent time getting to know each other: we had both been wounded by our experiences. Paul was recovering from his broken relationship; I found it hard to trust anybody, and I'd become very self-reliant. We became really good friends before we became lovers, but when we did, it was very precious.

Although so much had been done to me as a child that it would have been understandable if I had found sex difficult, with Paul it never was. I could very easily differentiate between what was done to me against my will, and what I entered into out of love. Sex with Paul had no connection with, or relationship to, the sex I had endured as a child. It was my decision, and it was with someone I loved and wanted to be with.

Even now that he knows everything that happened to me, Paul always reminds me that no matter what happened to me then, he was the first man who ever made *love* to me.

I had never been in love before, it was a completely new experience for me. Paul was the first person to treat me properly. As we got closer, and I got to know his children and we talked of my moving in with him, for the first time it seemed to me that I could have a normal life. However,

I felt it was really important that Paul never found out about my childhood: how could anyone ever love me if they knew what had happened to me? I really thought that what I had been through was so revolting that no man could possibly love me, or want to have sex with me, if he knew about all the abuse I had suffered.

I determined, at the very beginning of our relationship, that I would stick to the lies I had been telling for so many years: the fiction that I had a happy childhood with a loving mum and a good stepfather. I built up a whole fairytale about my early life. I buried the past, and created in its place the life I should have had. As a child, the bad things that happened to me were powerful enough to wipe out almost all my good memories: now it was the other way round, with the good times wiping out – or, at least, suppressing – all the bad memories.

It became all the more important to keep the fantasy going when I met Paul's family. He comes from a large, happy family, with six brothers and one sister. They may never have had much money but they always had lots of love for one another. When Paul or one of his brothers or sisters went out, their mum always said to them: 'Remember, my heart goes with you.'

Paul is very close to his brother Tony and Tony's wife Gail, and they all happily accepted me as Paul's new partner. The genuine affection they felt for each other, and the way they all adored their mum, made me envious, but also made me even more sure that I didn't want them to know the truth about my childhood.

Paul told me that when they were little they couldn't afford holidays, but their mum played a game with bits of paper in which they all imagined they were in exotic and adventurous places, such as on the Prairies with the cowboys and Indians. Their imagined journeys were as good as the real thing. I was struck by this and realised, with a deep feeling of regret, that nobody had ever played games like that with me when I was small.

Mum was happy enough to go along with my pretence that we were a normal family – she certainly never gave anything away which suggested that Heather and I had been abused. But Paul said from the very beginning that he didn't think she was a very devoted mum. On many occasions she and Rab would drive right past our flat to visit his family, not thinking to pop in to see us. I had to ring her and tell her that it was hurtful to me that she ignored us. You always had to tell Mum how to behave as a mother, it never came instinctively. On another occasion, Paul was surprised when I was mad at her for babysitting the child of a couple she knew. I told her she mustn't do it; I didn't ever want her to be left alone with a child. Fortunately Paul assumed it was because I was annoyed that she never babysat for us, and so he didn't ask any awkward questions.

He never suspected anything that came even close to what had happened. Although he said later that he felt she wasn't the best mum in the world, he certainly never suspected she was the worst. His mother, who knew my mum, described her as 'a party girl', and Paul could see that she was always more interested in her own pleasure than in caring for her daughters, but he had no idea how sinister that pleasure was. His mother also told him that I needed a lot of love, 'because she never got it from her own mother'.

In fact, I was so good at my act that on one occasion Paul went to Eastern Cemetery and cleaned up Billy's grave, as a special treat for me. He believed Billy had been a perfect stepdad to me, and he used to excuse Mum's behaviour because she had lost this great man from her life. He believed Billy's death had been a real tragedy for us all. I had to go with him later to see the grave and pretend to be really pleased. I felt like being sick, but I had to act the part, and thank Paul for being so good to 'my dad'. When I looked down at that plot of earth, where the three people I hated more than anything in the world rotted beneath, I had to shut off all my emotions and call on all my reserves as an actress. The only thing I was pleased about was that the grave was full, and no other innocent member of the family could be buried with them. Fortunately I was able to keep up the pretence of being happy about the grave being cleaned: I had developed a real split personality, and I was so well immersed in the world I had created that my act never faltered.

I got on well with Paul's children. It wasn't hard, as they are lovely boys and I've always loved kids. I was used to looking after Auntie Brenda's little girls, and Paul's two little boys took to me, quickly. The baby, Ryan, accepted me as his mum from the moment I moved into his life.

Young Paul was old enough to remember his own mum, and has always called me 'Dana' rather than 'Mum'. But I have been a mother to him in many ways, and on Mother's Day he always gives me a card. Their own mother did not see them, so there were not all the complications of having to arrange visits or share custody. It made life easier for us.

Taking on a baby was no problem for me, even though I realise, looking back, that I was only a kid myself. I had grown up very quickly because my childhood had been so terrible. And besides, in that area of Edinburgh, countless girls were pushing their babies in prams from the age of fourteen onwards. I never for one moment pretended that Ryan was my own baby, but there was status in being a young mother, and certainly no shame. I know it sounds stupid, but I loved showing him off.

I loved all the domesticity. I loved silly things, like doing the washing and making the dinners. Paul was a very hands-on dad, and Tony and Gail lived nearby and had children of the same sort of age, so I never felt isolated.

I began to feel an emotion that was quite alien to me: I was content. Of course, being newly in love with Paul, there were moments of great elation and wild happiness. But there was also a steady, deep, contentment, which came from the feeling that at last I was living a normal life. I realise now, looking back over my childhood, that there had been very, very few times in my life when I had ever felt content. Now, to my amazement, I was waking up each day in a glow of happiness. I had no idea that life could be so good.

Although I was no longer involved with my 'boyfriend abuser' he still kept in touch, trying to get back with me. Mum brought him round to see me, and Paul, and from the proprietorial way he behaved towards me, Paul was suspicious. I owned up to Paul that this man had been my lover for four years, and Paul was horrified when he learned that it had started when I was twelve. I hadn't told Paul anything about the other abuse I had suffered, but I was a little bit surprised by his reaction: on the scale of what had happened to me in life, my 'boyfriend abuser' had been the least of my problems. I suppose I was so inured to the fact that children were abused by adults that I didn't understand the shock and outrage that Paul felt. It was only as he talked to me that I really took on board that sexual abuse of children, even if they are twelve years old and willing, is fundamentally wrong and the very thought of it outrages normal decent people. Paul was even more horrified to find out that Mum knew all about this man's relationship with me. Rightly, he felt she should have been protecting me.

After talking to Paul I decided to go to the police to report this man. I made an appointment at a police station near to where my abuser lived, because I wanted to keep the allegations well away from my home area. Paul came with me and I made a statement, carefully avoiding any mention of my mum knowing or colluding in the abuse because I didn't want to risk the truth of my mum's abuse coming out. Obviously this meant I gave a very restricted version of what had happened.

I found the whole business very embarrassing, and it reawakened memories of the more serious abuse, which I was determined Paul should never find out about. Somehow, just talking about what I regarded as relatively unthreatening abuse made me feel dirty, as if I was in some way responsible for what had happened to me. I was worried that if I was not very careful, more than I wanted to tell would come out – and that if it did, I would lose Paul.

The police investigated, but after a few weeks they phoned to say they did not have enough evidence to proceed, and nothing happened. Now, in the light of everything else that has happened since, and with a lot more prosecutions possibly going ahead, he is being re-investigated. At the time, I was relieved that it was all going to be quietly dropped, even though I knew Paul was angry at this outcome, and I knew it was wrong he was getting away with it. I simply wanted all talk of child abuse to go away.

While all this was going on, the problems with my leg persisted. I was still having an open wound dressed every couple of days, and I still had no idea what it was or why it had happened to me. When I started going out with Paul I was very self-conscious about it. Although it was always covered by the dressing, underneath it really looked horrific.

On one visit to the hospital, when Paul dropped me off to have the dressing changed, the staff were more alarmed by it than usual. It looked particularly angry and sore, and, unusually, it was very painful. They told me they would have to take a sample to test. A young doctor broke the news to me that if the test showed that blood vessels had burst, it was likely they would have to amputate my leg below the knee.

I went into shock. This annoying and unsightly wound on my leg was suddenly something very serious. The only words I took in were that they would amputate the leg: my brain didn't really register that this would only happen if the test results were bad.

I rang Paul, crying down the phone, 'They're going to have to take my leg off.'

He drove back to the hospital immediately. I was in floods of tears when he found me, and he simply folded me into his arms and told me that he would love me no matter what happened, and he would still be with me even if I had to lose part of my leg. Looking back, that was the first time I knew how strong and supportive Paul could be: qualities I would come to rely on a great deal in years to come.

It was a very fraught and difficult week while I waited for the test results. I found it hard to sleep, and when I did drop off my dreams were vivid and scary. The night before we got the results I don't think I slept at all, and Paul very patiently kept the vigil with me, making me cups of coffee and telling me that, whatever the result, it wouldn't make any difference to his love for me.

We were at the hospital early, and we didn't have to wait long. Thank God, the biopsy had not shown any burst blood vessels, and my leg was safe. The nurses who gave me the results were delighted for me.

It was only when I changed hospitals that, while attending a diabetic clinic, a doctor asked to see my leg and told me I had Necrobiosis Lipoidica Diabeticorum. This is a rare skin disease that affects two in every thousand diabetics, usually young females. Although the cause is not known, it's believed to be related to the thickening and weakening of blood vessels.

So at least it had a name; I had a diagnosis and a reason for why I had developed it. But this didn't help a great deal: treatment remained much the same, with different creams and ointments being tried and none of them really improving things. By this time, the lesion down the front of my leg was about ten inches long and three inches wide, and looked as though someone had taken a huge scoop of flesh out of the leg. Eventually, after a few more months, the wound just dried up. I am left with a large scar, but it doesn't cause me any problems. I feel self-conscious about it in the summer, when my legs are bare, but compared to the risk of losing my leg that's nothing.

It is such a rare condition that my scar is a subject of great interest to any new doctors at the diabetic unit I attend. They always ask to see it and ask questions as most have only ever been able to read about it in their medical textbooks.

6

For Heather, the abuse at the hands of our grandfather went on and on. I had no idea it was continuing. Looking back, I think I was so preoccupied with surviving myself that I had little spare time or resources to worry about anything else. Because Heather never spoke about it, I had no clue. And, because she was so vulnerable, I assumed everyone would feel like I did towards her, and look after her. I was still too young to realise that her vulnerability actually made her an easier target for predators.

It was much worse for her at Granddad's hands than it ever was for me. I only had to endure his abuse for a couple of years: for Heather it went on until she was sixteen. Although Granddad King would definitely be the worst of the men who abused us, for Heather the longest-lasting abuse came from Granddad. And, unlike in my case, it wasn't only he who was involved.

Granddad introduced Heather to George Jamieson. He was a very unpleasant character, a man who had been an associate of Granddad's for more than thirty years. He was living at Granddad's and Nana's house in 1970 when he was arrested and tried for murdering a nineteen-year-old girl on some wasteland in the Castle Wynd area of old Edinburgh. He said he had met her in a pub, while she was out with friends, and when she left the pub with him he killed her by kicking her on the head and body, stamping on her, and tying a ligature around her neck. It was a particularly brutal murder. Mum was a small child living at home at the time of that murder. She later said she was raped by Jamieson on a regular basis when she was a child, which I'm certain is true – if her own father, Granddad, was raping her, I'm sure he was allowing his pal to do the same.

After serving his sentence Jamieson drifted back into Granddad's orbit, although I don't think he lived at the house again. He was always round there, but I only saw him a few times as, now I'd left home, I rarely went to visit my grandparents. After Nana died in 1996 I had only very loose contact with Granddad. I was caught up in my own life with Paul, so it was easy for me to avoid seeing him without anyone thinking it was odd. When Paul once asked me why I didn't go to see my grandfather more often, I just said I didn't like him for drinking so much, which Paul accepted.

Jamieson was small, bald and ugly, with a stupid comb-over hairstyle, a few long threads of hair vainly combed across the top of his head. To me, a teenager, he looked very old, but he was probably in his sixties. He had children of his own, one of whom was a girl about the same age as Heather. When Heather was thirteen, Jamieson raped her at Granddad's house, although I had no idea of this at the time. I only found out about it after the police investigation began.

When Heather was sixteen Jamieson ran away with her, taking her with him to live in Arbroath, a seaside town about ninety miles north of Edinburgh.

By this time, Heather had also been diagnosed as diabetic. She was sixteen when she began to drink a lot of liquid, and she seemed generally unwell. Knowing the signs of the illness because of her experience with me and Billy, Mum took Heather to the doctors, who, after testing her blood-sugar level, sent her straight to hospital. Unlike me, she didn't have to stay in overnight; she spent a few hours in the diabetic clinic, then came home with her insulin. Heather understands that she has to take her injections regularly, and most of the time she does it herself, but I have to keep an eye on her, to make sure she's keeping it on track.

By the time she was sixteen she looked quite grown up. She and I don't look a bit alike. I'm skinny and fair haired, she's slightly chubby and dark haired. In fact, I'm the only member of the family who doesn't have dark hair: both Mum and my real dad Tam have dark hair. I can't say I mind not having much in common with them all.

When I say Jamieson 'ran away' with Heather, I don't think Mum objected. Looking after Heather was a problem for Mum. It interfered with her drinking and her relationship with Rab, and I think she was quite happy to have Heather taken off her hands. She told me Heather had gone. She said that she and Jamieson had come to the flat where Mum and Rab were living, and Heather had taken her things and left. I don't think Mum made any effort to stop them.

Paul was shocked and very disturbed when he heard about it: he didn't think Jamieson was the right person to be looking after a vulnerable girl like Heather. I was slower to react: again, the amorality of my childhood made it harder for me to see, in such a black-and-white way as Paul did, how wrong the situation was. Also, Paul knew more about Jamieson's history of extreme violence, having lived in the area where he had committed the murder.

Jamieson was more than forty years older than Heather, and Paul said he was 'a paedophile'. I'd heard the word before, and I knew that the men who abused us as children were paedophiles, but because Heather was now over the legal age to have sex, I thought all that was behind us. But Paul was absolutely right, however, because Heather still had the mental age of a child and was in no position to make decisions about her own life without a great deal of help.

We were very worried about her – and with good cause. We didn't know it at the time, but Jamieson was using her as a prostitute: he was making her go with men, complete strangers to her, in return for money or cans of beer. He was a very heavy drinker, so this arrangement supported his habit. He was also heavy-handed with her: he used to hit her regularly.

Over the months she was with him, we heard from different people various rumours about how Heather was being treated and we learned a bit more from Heather herself when she occasionally managed to escape back to Edinburgh, usually after Jamieson had kicked her out on to the streets. More than once, Mum had to persuade someone to drive her up to Arbroath, a round trip of 180 miles, to rescue Heather. While Mum never protected Heather from the Kings, she at least felt she had some control over it but, in this instance, she knew Jamieson well enough to know that he was actually capable of murder. We always tried to make Heather stay, but every time Jamieson would come looking for her and drag her back to Arbroath. One of his family was also physically abusive to Heather – publicly attacking her. The very thought of Heather being treated like this makes my blood run cold and tears well up in my eyes. I am much more easily upset by the idea of Heather being mistreated than I am by anything that happened to me, because she is so helpless and unable to stand up for herself.

Once when she was in Arbroath, Heather ran out of insulin, and Jamieson wouldn't let her go to the doctor to get another prescription. She ended up in hospital, in a coma. I only heard about it later, but I was furious: the one thing I have always tried to drill into Heather is that she has to take her illness seriously.

She also became pregnant when she was sixteen, and had a miscarriage. She didn't tell me this until many years later. Being Heather, always living in the present, she doesn't seem to have any deep regrets about losing the baby, and if she had given birth it would have made our complicated lives even more difficult, so it was probably just as well.

It was only when Jamieson brought her back to Edinburgh permanently, when she was twenty, that we heard more details about the way she had been treated in Arbroath. Paul was very suspicious of Jamieson, who we heard was bragging about the cruelties he inflicted on Heather. To find out more, and to try to collect evidence against him, Paul acted in a friendly way towards Jamieson, inviting him round to our flat for a drink. Jamieson believed we had no problem with him being with Heather. Unknown to him, Paul had set up a video camera and recorded everything that was said.

It was shocking stuff. Paul had to act his way through the evening, encouraging Jamieson to speak. After everything that he poured out on the video, our suspicions about him ill treating Heather were no longer in doubt. Paul insisted that she came to live with us, and he went to the police to tell them everything he had heard. Jamieson was arrested.

After holding him in custody over a weekend, the police released him on the Monday morning, without charge. They said Paul's video wouldn't stand as evidence, because it was 'entrapment'. In other words, they said Paul had trapped Jamieson into saying the things he had admitted. Jamieson had served a life sentence, and anyone released after serving life is on licence for the rest of their lives; they can be recalled to prison at any time if they break the law. So we were horrified that he was not held for longer or charged with something.

Heather stayed with us, relieved to be away from him – she has lived with us ever since, and Paul and I have done everything in our power to keep her safe and happy, although it hasn't always been easy.

We had made a terrible enemy in Jamieson, and he was determined to get Heather back – at any cost.

It was soon after this that Heather started talking about Granddad abusing her. When she first said it, I went into shock. I had never even considered that he might be doing it to her as well. I was disgusted with him for abusing Heather, but at the same time I was also terrified that it would come out that he had abused me as well. By this time I was happily caught up in my life with Paul, determined to keep up the myth of my happy childhood. I was seriously scared of losing him.

At first I simply shut off from it, tried to ignore what Heather was saying in the hope that it would go away. I wanted Heather to shut up, to leave the past alone. Once things started coming out, where would it end? In my mind, I was still part and parcel of the abuse, I felt guilty about it as though I had asked for it, and not been forced into it. It's a very hard emotion to explain, but I did not feel like an innocent victim, I felt tainted.

Obviously, after Heather's accusation, Paul asked me about Granddad. All I would say was, 'He's always been a good granddad to me.'

I'm ashamed to admit that I even tried to suggest that

Heather didn't know what she was talking about. I came very close to calling her a liar. I was covering up for him, trying to make out that Heather was imagining it all. Of course, I knew she wasn't. But I felt my whole life was so precarious. I genuinely felt that all my happiness would come crashing down around me, and I'd lose everything.

Paul was still very upset about it. From the moment he met Heather, he has been protective of her, and sometimes, to my shame, more worried about her than I have been. After everything that had happened to her with Jamieson, Paul insisted that we went to see Granddad and confront him. He was still living in the Muirhouse area, on his own since Nana's death.

Of course, he denied it: he was probably very relieved that it was only Heather making the allegations, not me, because it was easy to argue that Heather didn't understand things. I had hoped we could leave it at that, but ever since Heather had mentioned it, the memories that I had been suppressing kept forcing their way back into my mind. I wanted to leave it where it was, in an unopened box at the back of my consciousness, but Heather talking about it meant the box lid was prised open.

I continued to push the memories away, and for some time we lived a very normal life. There was a safe and comforting rhythm to it: I took Young Paul to school in the mornings, looked after Ryan, shopped, cooked and cleaned. I was very content: this was the life that I was fighting so hard to preserve, and it was for this that I struggled to keep such tormenting memories at bay. But they insisted on surfacing: I spent many nights lying awake while Paul slept next to me, worrying about it all and feeling as consumed by the threat of the truth coming out as I had been by the threat of Billy's night-time visits.

One of the things that puzzles me most about my mother is how she attracted such a succession of paedophiles. It's as if she walked around with a neon light flashing on her head, which said 'Welcome All Paedophiles'. She didn't take care of herself, and she drank and smoked too much, but even so she was a reasonably attractive woman. She could, you would think, have found herself a normal bloke. But with only the odd exception, the majority of the men she hooked up with all shared a perverse sexual interest in young children. Everyone can make a mistake and hitch up with the wrong partner, but her mistakes were repeated time and time again. Although I have never thought she would initiate abuse if she was on her own, I think I have to reluctantly accept that she, too, has an unhealthy appetite for children. If not, why didn't she stop the whole thing? If she was in too deep with the Kings, and found she could not get out, why did she carry on associating with paedophiles after they died?

She even became engaged to Rab, although the relationship ended before he went to prison. He and Mum went on holiday to Scarborough, and in the tourist attraction, Flamingo Land, he proposed on stage to her, and she accepted.

When the girl he abused revealed what had happened

to her, Rab confessed straightaway. Not that this helped the girl much as she has struggled to hold her life together ever since. At the time of his arrest, he was also interviewed by the police about abusing Heather, who had been living with him and Mum. But that was not proceeded with for lack of evidence. Despite this, Mum spoke up for him to the police and continued to live with him, and Heather moved in with Nana and Granddad. At the time I thought this was a good thing; it was before Heather had made any allegations against Granddad.

Rab and Mum split up after a row which was nothing to do with his pending court case, and his ex-partner's brother, Alan Kay, helped Mum move out of his home. She'd kept her own flat in Pennywell all the time she was living with Rab, so Alan drove Mum and her belongings back there. He ended up moving in with her straightaway. It turned out that for some time he'd been telling her that he could look after her better than Rab could.

At this stage I was obviously still pretending to Paul that she was a great mother, and she used to come round to visit us with Alan. Initially I thought Alan was quite good news. I liked him better than I had liked Rab. Alan was small and thin, with a slight hump, a bald head, and he always wore a rain jacket. He had a job, doing deliveries, and because he worked he had a bit of money to spare. They bought things for the home together, including lots of electrical goods like televisions, hi-fis and computers. Alan had two or three grown-up children from a previous relationship. He also seemed to not mind Mum's urge to move home on a regular basis – they had several flats over the next few years.

I felt uncomfortable about him being around the boys, but I wasn't sure whether I was being paranoid or not. Alan seemed happier clowning around and playing with the children than being with the adults. I'm so sensitive to the threat of child abuse that I'm always in danger of over-reacting, but I determined never to leave him alone with our children.

Paul wondered whether he was 'not the full deck', and there was something missing in his brain that made him incapable of talking with adults. Paul would say to him, 'Leave the kids to their games and come sit with us, Alan.' But after a while he'd drift back to whatever game the boys were playing.

What worries us now, in retrospect, is that when he and Mum lived together they used to babysit other people's children. Whenever I heard about it, I tried to stop it, but it was hard to do so without revealing why. When Paul asked why I was so keen that they shouldn't look after children I said, 'She doesn't care about children and he acts daft around them.' Luckily for me, Paul accepted this.

As far as we know, no harm was done and Alan Kay has never been convicted of paedophilia. But we can never be sure with my mum; how can anybody know, if the children said nothing? And that, as I know only too well, is what most abused children do: they say nothing.

7

Heather's mobile phone rang. She glanced at the number on the screen, began trembling and wordlessly held the phone out to me. Her fear told me who it was.

'Hullo?' I said.

A gruff voice on the other end spoke: 'I'm going to kill you. I'm going to cut your body into little pieces and throw it into the dock. I'm watching you. Don't think Paul can protect you . . .'

I cut the call off. It was Jamieson. He was a formidable enemy and, after we had gone to the police about his behaviour towards Heather, he unleashed a reign of terror against us.

In one of his threatening calls, he told us that he was quite happy to do another life sentence for killing Heather.

'I've done it once, I'll do it again. It would be a pleasure.

Don't ever think I'm frightened of the law. Prison doesn't bother me.'

We changed Heather's mobile phone number, but he would ring mine, or the house phone instead. Sometimes he shouted and yelled about what he was going to do; other times, more worryingly, he spoke with quiet menace. I had no doubt that he meant what he said, and I was worried sick about Heather's safety.

She was terrified, and I bought her a panic alarm which she constantly wore round her neck. It was a device that would make a loud shrieking noise if she pressed it to hopefully bring help to her if he ever approached her in the street. Thankfully she never needed to use it, but that's largely because she hardly ever left the flat. If she wanted to go to the garage across the road to buy something from the small supermarket there, we watched her from the window the whole time. If she went to a friend's house, we drove her there and picked her up later. We took care to never leave her on her own, and our door was constantly locked. She lost her freedom completely, and in many ways we lost ours as well, but she bravely stuck to her promise not to go back to him.

Paul recorded the threats, but even though we told the police, nothing happened. The fact that he had served a life sentence, and was therefore on licence, seemed to make no difference. We were disappointed he wasn't arrested by the police, as it would have made Heather feel more secure.

Paul was not frightened by the threats, and his strength made me feel much better. But we were both concerned about the effect it was having on Heather. We were leading our normal lives, Paul running his furniture-removal business with his brother Tony, and me looking after the boys, so we had the chance to forget about Jamieson, at least for some of the time. But poor Heather was practically housebound, and always very afraid.

The worst night came just two or three weeks after the weekend when Jamieson was held and questioned by the police. We were in the middle of moving from our flat in Ferry Road, in the Muirhouse area, to a new flat in the Hutchison area, and Paul and I were spending some time painting and decorating it, getting it ready for the family. It's a council flat, and when we took possession of it, it was in a bad state, and needed cleaning and decorating throughout.

One evening, we'd left Heather looking after the children. Mum and Alan were also there. They had come round to visit, a rare thing for Mum, and they were there when Paul and I arrived back at the flat, at about ten o'clock, tired and paint-spattered, and looking forward to an early night.

A woman associated with Jamieson phoned to say that she wanted to call round to collect a DVD which she said we had, and which belonged to her. We agreed she could come over, because we didn't regard her as a threat, and there were a few of us there. She arrived with a friend of hers and they sounded friendly and reasonable on the doorstep. Once they came into the flat, however, their attitude changed. One of them started shouting abuse at

Heather, and trying to attack her. Paul opened the door to chuck them out – then quickly slammed it shut because a crowd of youths, who we later realised were drunk, were surging up the stairwell, yelling abuse at us. Our flat in Ferry Road was on the first floor of a three-floor building, with communal stairwells. Although there are doors to the stairwells, there is no intercom system and they open easily. Jamieson was not amongst them, but he had sent them to attack us. We heard later that he paid for a party at his flat, with loads of drink for the youngsters, then fired them all up to come round to get his revenge on us. He was too smart to be caught there with them. The two women were just the advance party, clearing the way for the main assault.

We were now trapped in the flat with a hoard of people outside, some of them attacking our front door with hammers and bicycle chains. They were screaming and yelling, bricks were being thrown at our windows, and the wood of the front door was splintering and bowing under the force of the attack. Paul had to put all his weight behind it to prevent it giving way, and he narrowly missed being stabbed when someone thrust a long knife at him through the letterbox. I had already rung the police, but the wait for them to arrive, which was probably no more than ten minutes, seemed like an eternity.

Inside, the two women were screaming, swearing and running around dementedly, sweeping ornaments off shelves. They threw the computer to the floor. I ran to the bedroom to check on Ryan, who was only five at the time, and Young Paul, who was eleven. The only plan I could formulate amidst the mayhem was to get all of us into one room and to barricade ourselves in. The children were terrified, whimpering and crying, and I was doing my best to reassure them when I heard a scream from Heather, who was in the living room.

I rushed back to see blood pouring down her face from a deep cut on her head. Alan, who had tried to pull the two women off Heather, was now under attack himself. I grabbed a jacket, the only thing I could find, and held it against the wound on Heather's head to staunch the blood flow, and as I did so one of the women ran past me and punched me in my face: I ended up with a painfully swollen black eye.

At last the police sirens could be heard, and the mob on the stairs made a run for it. The police had blockaded both ends of the street, so they were trapped. A total of thirty-three people were arrested and cautioned that night. When I looked out of the window, I could see the police standing at the bottom of the stairwell: I don't think they realised that two of the aggressors were still inside our flat. I yelled down, 'Can we have some help up here – my sister's losing a lot of blood.'

With that, two of the policemen came dashing up. They arrested the two women who were both so drunk that when the police appeared they attacked them, too. There was a struggle as the police tried to restrain them – I remember that in the confusion one of the women crashed into my large fish tank, which was in the hall. Luckily, she didn't break it. By this time the children were screaming hysterically, and I was doing my best to comfort them while still looking after Heather. Mum was in a corner of the room, and had managed not to get hurt.

An ambulance arrived as the two women were arrested. Luckily, although the split on the back of Heather's head was pouring blood, it was superficial and the paramedics were able to clean it and treat it without taking Heather to hospital. Within half an hour of the whole ordeal starting it was all over, but living through it seemed like a lifetime. I had never experienced such out-of-control violence on this scale, and, although I realise it could have been a lot worse, I felt in shock. We were all pumping adrenalin, and none of us, not even the children, were able to settle. Ryan was OK because he was so young and didn't really understand what was happening. But Young Paul was traumatised, crying and clinging to me. Heather, too, needed a lot of attention: she was sobbing and shaking, and when she finally stopped crying she sat quietly, rocking herself.

The next few hours were spent clearing up and calming everyone down. There was no substantial damage to the flat, just a few broken ornaments and a lot of mess where they had overturned furniture and strewn papers across the floor. The main task was to reassure the children, and to try to reintroduce some normality to them. We could not stay there that night, so we all went to stay with Tony and Gail. The council workmen turned up very promptly to put steel shutters on the door, to secure the flat, but as the other flat was almost ready we never moved back to the Ferry Road flat.

Eventually, a few months later, the two women came up in court charged with assault on Heather and on a police officer. They pleaded not guilty, so Paul, Heather and I were called as witnesses. The case was heard at the Sheriff's Court, and it was the first time I had ever been in a courtroom. It was over in one day, and they were found guilty and given a community service sentence. I have not seen either of them since.

The day after the attack, we moved to the new flat at Hutchison, but escaping to another area didn't mean we were safe. Just a few days later Paul's removal van was set on fire. It was the evening and we were at home when we heard a commotion and a loud crackling noise coming from outside. When we looked out of the window we saw the van going up in flames. It was a massive blaze, lighting up the whole street. The police were never able to find out who did it – or, to be more accurate, to prove who did it. One of the first things Paul had done when we moved in, because we knew we were still targets of Jamieson and his mob, was to rig up our own security camera trained on the street and, on the film, you can clearly see a young man running away from the blaze. We have no doubt who it is, and that he was part of the same campaign waged against us by Jamieson, but the footage is not clear enough for a prosecution.

The furniture van was insured, but Paul and I both agreed that he should not buy another one, as it would be too dangerous to drive around so conspicuously.

The harassment continued. Shortly after this, a replica gun was fired at our window. I was at home with Paul and the boys when we heard a loud crack against the window. Luckily, the glass did not shatter. Again we had CCTV film footage of the person who did it, but again he could not be seen clearly enough to be identified. On a couple of occasions there were anonymous phone calls to the police accusing Paul of some crime. He could easily prove that he wasn't there when the crime was carried out, but he still had to cope with the hassle and humiliation of being questioned about it by the police.

We also received lots of threatening phone calls. 'Is that Dana? Did you get any bargains at Asda this morning? Did the kids enjoy their wee play on the swings this afternoon down at the park?' It was a man's voice, a soft monotone, and it really spooked me to realise that I was being watched and that my movements were being recorded. I made a point of always parking in the busiest part of the car park, and I never went into the park with the children unless there were plenty of other people there. I tried not to let the children pick up my anxiety, but all the time, even as I stood at the school gates, I was looking around, trying to spot my stalker.

Sometimes it would be Paul's phone he called. 'Paul, you are a lucky man. I really like that blue top Dana was wearing today when I saw her at the supermarket . . .'

We increased Heather's security, refusing to allow her out of the house at all unless accompanied by someone big and strong, like Paul or Tony.

It was not until Jamieson died of cancer, about two

years ago, that Heather finally felt completely secure. He was under investigation by the police at the time, for his treatment of Heather when she lived with him, but also for taking part in raping her, with other men, when she was thirteen. He had given a statement that was going to be used in evidence against Granddad. He didn't admit carrying out paedophile offences with Granddad, but he was prepared to say he knew what Granddad had been doing with Heather. On his deathbed he told the police, 'Tell Paul he got me – but I'll never do a day in jail.'

I always badly wanted my own baby. It was not that I didn't love Ryan and Young Paul, but I had always longed for my own children, and had done since I was a child. I knew I could do a far better job than my mum and, in some ways, I felt it would make amends for my own lost childhood. I didn't want to be like some of the single mums in our area who had babies by men they hardly knew. So as soon as I was in a steady relationship with Paul, and knew that we would stay together, I wanted to have his baby. Every time I got pregnant, however, something went wrong. I had three miscarriages in those first years that I was with Paul.

The first pregnancy came very early in our relationship, and – much as I always wanted a baby – I knew it was too soon. I was shocked, and so was Paul. I hadn't even realised I was pregnant. I was in hospital because of a complication with my diabetes when a nurse casually said, 'Do you realise you're pregnant?'

Before we had time to get used to the idea, I started to bleed heavily, and had really bad pains in my stomach. I went back to hospital for a scan and they told me I'd had a very early miscarriage. I felt a mixture of relief and disappointment. My body was obviously already preparing for a baby, because even though we both agreed it was much the best outcome so soon in our relationship, I had a hollow, empty feeling afterwards, which made me feel terribly sad.

The next pregnancy came a few years into the relationship, and this was different because we both really wanted to start our own family by this time. When I suspected I was pregnant, I went to the doctor. The pregnancy test was positive! I was so excited and happy. But the joy was short-lived. When I started to have a pain in my stomach I was booked in for an early scan. By the day of the scan the pains were severe, and I was very worried. I was sure I was losing my baby. I knew by the look on the face of the woman who was doing the scan that there was something seriously wrong, and she went out of the room to bring someone else in to talk to me.

'I'm afraid I have bad news. There's no heartbeat,' she said, very gently.

I burst into tears. I was so upset and I was still in agony. The woman doctor explained that the baby had died in the womb, and I would either miscarry naturally or they would operate to remove the foetus. In fact, the baby miscarried that same day. Paul was very supportive and looked after me, comforting me in my distress. But I could not tell him my real fear: that the abuse I had suffered had damaged me, and that I would never be able to hold on to a baby.

The third miscarriage was almost an exact copy of the second one, except that this time the baby did not come away completely and I had to have a 'd and c' (dilatation and curettage) operation afterwards to clear my womb. It was even more upsetting, because this time I didn't have the acute pain to warn me that something was going wrong, and when I went for the scan I was still excited and happy.

After this, my worries magnified. I was convinced that I would never manage to have a baby, and I was now sure that the abuse I had suffered as a very small child could well have done permanent damage, preventing me from being able to carry a baby to full term. Of course, I could not share this fear with anyone: neither the doctors, nurses, diabetic nurse nor, most of all, Paul. It was my own private torment.

I *do* now know that I have suffered some internal damage. I have a twisted small bowel, and I also have problems with the large bowel. Heather, too, has bowel problems. I don't think it is a coincidence: we were both abused anally for so long, when our bodies were far too small and underdeveloped. It's impossible that this couldn't have caused long-term damage.

I am also prone to bouts of sickness, and am often unwell. On several occasions I was so sick I was taken into hospital. Tests were carried out, but the doctors never seemed to get to the root of what was wrong with me.

Having Type One diabetes also means that any pregnancy

is very risky. If you are diabetic you are very closely monitored throughout your pregnancy, and if your blood sugars are too high you may be advised to have an abortion because the risk that the baby will not develop properly is very great if the diabetes is not being successfully managed.

I tried not to think about the possibility that I would never have children. Having a baby was the one thing I had always dreamed of, and for so long I had planned how I would bring up my own family. It was a dream I really didn't want to let go of. But after my third miscarriage, I was beginning to feel quietly desperate. It seemed so unjust: Mum had given birth to me and Heather with no problems, and she had been completely unfit to bring us up. I knew I would be a good mother, that my children would always come first in my life, that I was in a strong relationship and would be able to give my children a doting father.

The move to Hutchison made me long for a baby even more. It is a much better area than the one we left behind. At first I actually felt out of place, as though I didn't belong in such a respectable neighbourhood. Living in Muirhouse you watched your back when you walked to the shops, but you also met so many people who chatted to you.

But I soon began to appreciate the peace and calm of the area, and I felt it would be a great place to raise a growing family. Our flat was on the middle floor of a block of three, and the gardens around the flats were well cared for and really attractive, with lots of grass and flowers beds. There was a man up the street who won competitions for keeping such a beautiful and special garden.

Ryan settled in well at the local school, which is just along the road. Young Paul also went to school there, but when he reached twelve, and it was time to go to high school, he decided he would rather be with his old pals, so he caught the bus every day back to Muirhouse, where he went to Craigroyston school, the same one I attended. Life was good, although, like every family, we had our problems. Paul and I were both very worried when Ryan fell and slashed his face with a deep cut running from his nose to his mouth. We got him to hospital, where a plastic surgeon had to stitch his face. He did a really good job, though: if you look closely you can see a faint scar, but it really doesn't show.

It was a very sad time when Paul's mum died in the summer of 2001. She was an inspiration to me: despite any problems she faced, her love for her children never faltered. In the time I had known Paul I had become close to her. Her children adored her: when she was dying they clubbed together, selling some of their things, to raise the money to send her to Lourdes the Catholic shrine in France. In the final days of her life we saw a lot of her, and she was so comfortable with me that she allowed me to bathe her. I lit candles, and tried to make the whole experience as relaxing as possible for her. Sadly, she didn't live to see me fulfil my ambition to become a mother myself.

I was twenty-three – old for a girl from a tough area of Edinburgh – when I eventually became pregnant with my first son, Jordan. I was very careful throughout the pregnancy, looking after myself, attending the pregnancy diabetes clinic regularly, resting, eating well, and generally doing everything possible to make sure this pregnancy worked.

Paul looked after me. He didn't know anything about my deep fears that my body was damaged, but he knew how upset I had been by the miscarriages, and how important it was that this pregnancy went to term. But it was not easy, as I was constantly sick and lost a lot of weight. When we moved to Hutchison I had been transferred for my diabetic care to Edinburgh Royal Infirmary, and the doctor there was determined to get to the bottom of my general debility and sickness. He did a lot more tests and investigations and, eventually, he arranged for a liver specialist to see me, although at the time I wasn't told why.

While I was pregnant with Jordan, I had to remind Mum again that I was her daughter, and that I was carrying her first grandchild. Paul's brother Tony and his wife Gail were giving us things for the baby, Auntie Brenda and Uncle Bilko were delighted, we were all getting excited. But Mum never even asked me how I was feeling. When I told her I thought she should be taking more interest, she just said, 'What do you want me to buy you?'

In the end, I went to the market with her and Alan and they bought me some baby clothes and cot blankets. It was as if she had no instinct for how to behave, no genuine feeling. If you prompted her, she would do it. Otherwise she was numb to any emotion.

I loved being pregnant, I felt really happy, especially when I felt Jordan kicking inside me. It was everything I had ever wanted, and I was thrilled to watch my tummy expand, knowing that I finally had my dream come true, my own baby.

I was, of course, very anxious in case something went wrong, even after I got beyond the critical three-month stage of the pregnancy. I never for one moment took it for granted that I would give birth to a normal, healthy baby. Every night I was on the phone to Auntie Brenda, going through with her any little twinges or fears that I'd had during the day.

Unfortunately, I fell and broke my ankle during the pregnancy. It was so stupid: I was getting out of the car and I tripped, twisting my ankle as I fell. My sense of balance was probably disrupted by my new shape and weight, but I still felt like such a fool. I spent a few weeks hobbling around on crutches, but luckily I was out of plaster by the time I went into labour.

Towards the end of the pregnancy I was going to the diabetes pregnancy clinic at the Edinburgh Royal Infirmary every two days for monitoring. Four days before the baby was due I was feeling very ill and I was vomiting a lot. When they tested me they found that my ketone levels were very high. Ketones are compounds in the blood which are broken down to create energy, but which in some cases, as with diabetes, cannot be dealt with by the body.

I could see the medical staff going into a huddle to talk about me, and the midwife came back to my bedside and said, 'The good news is, we're going to start you off. The bad news is, it's in half an hour.'

'Can't I go home first?' I asked.

The answer was no. Luckily, I already had my bag packed, and just had to fetch it from the car. Then I was taken to the labour ward, where I was set up with a drip to induce labour.

I rang Paul and Mum, and they both came. Mum stayed with me throughout the labour. I was very lucky: I had no pain, I wasn't aware of any contractions, and the midwife who checked on me was amazed to find that I was well on: my cervix was already eight centimetres dilated. The midwife who was monitoring the baby's heartbeat raised the alarm that his condition was becoming unstable, and his heart rate was dropping, so I had to have an emergency Caesarean. I was given an epidural injection in my spine so that I was awake during the birth. Paul came in to the theatre with me, and was there when our healthy seven pounds three ounces son was delivered. Mum waited outside, but came in to see him as soon as it was all over. She was acting the part of a loving mum really well, and I was pleased because this was the fairytale I wanted.

I had already chosen his name: Jordan. Paul didn't like it at first, and we had a bit of a squabble over it. But I was determined: I'd known for ages that if I had a boy he would be called Jordan.

When a diabetic mother gives birth, it is really important that the baby is fed regularly to stabilise the blood sugars. The night after Jordan was born I woke at four in the morning and realised immediately that his cot was not beside my bed. I jumped up and, despite my Caesarean stitches, I ran to the nursery in a blind panic.

'Where's Jordan? Where's my baby?' I cried.

'It's OK – we've got him here and we're just giving him a feed,' one of the nurses told me.

I went back to bed, but just over an hour later they woke me again to say Jordan was being taken to the special baby unit, because he was having difficulty feeding. I rang Paul, crying my eyes out. I was able to go with Jordan when they took him, but it was a long walk from the ward to the unit, and I felt so far away from him that night. The staff gave me a photo of him to take back with me, which helped, but it felt horrible, seeing all the other mothers with their babies next to their beds.

I spent every day at the baby unit, where Jordan was fed through a tube for the first three days. I felt very panicky, imagining all sorts of problems. Even though the staff reassured me, I found it hard to sleep, and I wished I could have spent all night in the special baby unit. Happily, he did well, and we were allowed home from hospital after five days. I recovered well from the operation, and Jordan quickly established good feeding routines.

I loved having him; he more than lived up to my expectations. At first I could hardly believe he was really mine: it took a while to sink in that I had a baby, and that he was a perfectly healthy baby.

I wouldn't let anyone do anything for him: I was the only one who could feed him, bath him, dress him. I got up with him in the middle of the night, every night. Paul volunteered to look after him to give me a break, but at first I was too possessive about him. It didn't take long before the exhaustion kicked in, though, and I was glad to accept Paul's help.

After Jordan was born, Paul took him up to Easter Road Cemetery to 'introduce' him to his step-grandfather, Billy. The very thought of it sickened me, but I could not find any way of stopping Paul without telling him how I really felt about Billy. Paul told me how he took flowers, and spoke to Billy at the graveside, telling him about Jordan and saying, 'I love your daughter as much as you loved her, and I'll look after her as well as you would if you were alive today.'

Paul insisted we make 'William' Jordan's second name, in memory of Billy. I tried to persuade him against it, telling him that his mother would not have liked it; she was a devout Roman Catholic, and 'King Billy' is a figure of hate to Scottish Catholics. But Paul just argued, 'We're naming him after a good man, and that's what's important.'

In the end I said I would agree to him being named William after my Uncle Bilko. Paul thought it was strange that I didn't want it to be after Billy, but he accepted it, especially as Uncle Bilko is Jordan's godfather.

The love I felt for Jordan was overwhelming. I would cradle him in my arms and whisper to him, 'I'll never, ever, let anyone hurt you.' Tears would form in my eyes when I remembered that I, too, had been this small once, and my mum should have felt the same way about me. I had always known it was unnatural of her to be cruel to her own children, but holding my baby in my arms made me even more painfully aware of the reality, of the bleakness of my own childhood.

But, when I pushed those thoughts away, everything seemed pretty much perfect in our lives – apart from my health.

The sickness and weight loss became worse, and I was taken into hospital for a liver biopsy: they had not wanted to do it when I was pregnant. The result showed that my liver is scarred and enlarged, symptoms normally caused by heavy, long-term drinking. I've only ever drunk heavily for those few weeks after Billy's death when Mum would bribe me with bottles of vodka; I've never been exposed to chemicals such as cleaning fluids on a long-term basis; and I don't have hepatitis. Which rules out all the usual causes. There is nothing that can be done about it, but it does give me a lot of pain, for which I am prescribed painkillers, and at times my tummy swells up quite noticeably.

It seems that it is just something I will always have to live with.

8

It was when I was pregnant that, by chance, my father came back into my life.

'Dana, Dana!'

I was walking through the Wester Hailes shopping centre with Paul, smugly enjoying being very pregnant with Jordan, and getting a real thrill from buying bits and pieces for my baby. It was a rare chance for me and Paul to escape the rest of the family and to wander around together, planning for the baby and feeling quietly excited about the future.

'Dana!'

I turned to see who was calling me. I recognised Tam instantly, although his appearance had changed and it had been many years. I was surprised to see him sober, neatly dressed, and walking along with a pleasant-looking woman and three little boys.

He was very friendly, and seemed delighted that I was pregnant. He introduced us to his partner and sons, and he talked about them affectionately, like a caring dad. I had only seen him once or twice since the time he had visited me in hospital when I was seven. When I was about nineteen he had been living in the Broomhouse area, close to where Mum and Heather were living, and Heather had been round to his house a couple of times. He was with a different woman then, and was still drinking heavily, so I wouldn't have anything to do with him. He soon dropped the connection with Heather.

But I was pleased to see him now. After everything I had been through at the hands of my stepfather, Billy, I had occasionally wondered whether life would have been better with Tam around. I was sure it couldn't have been worse. Meeting him, he seemed OK, sober and taking his responsibilities towards his little boys seriously. He and Paul had a chat, and they got on – Paul, too, formed the opinion that Tam was a decent guy.

We exchanged addresses and arranged to go round and see them. The visit went well. He was still drinking, but he wasn't such an idiot for drink as he had been. I got the impression that he had turned his life around, perhaps because, a few years earlier, he had been sentenced to a year in jail for drink driving and giving a false identity to the police. He had accepted he was an alcoholic after that case, and had been trying to curb his drinking.

I got on well with his partner and the kids. As we left, he invited us back for dinner. He finally seemed like a real dad. He told me how special I was to him, and it felt good; it was what I had always wanted to hear from him. I knew I was special to Paul and his side of the family, but there was nobody on my side, apart from Heather and Auntie Brenda, who really cared about me. Perhaps I was being naïve, but I had high expectations of Tam. I knew he had a drink problem, but I thought that underneath it he was a good man and that he loved me.

We started to see quite a lot of my dad. I was bowled over by how much alike we were. It sounds silly, I suppose, to anyone who has had both of their parents with them throughout their lives, but little things like finding out that Tam liked eating his toast cold – like me – and that I discovered he and I liked the same Shania Twain songs, meant a great deal to me. I could see a connection between us, I could work out little things I must have inherited from him.

Tam came up to see us as soon as I came home with the baby and he seemed to be thrilled with Jordan. He sometimes stayed overnight with us, and once I'd relaxed enough to let others help me with Jordan, he'd be up early, bathing and dressing him. The other boys, Ryan and Young Paul, got on with him too, and Paul and he became good mates. Best of all for me and Heather, he told us he loved us, and that we were his beautiful daughters. If you have never had a parent tell you they love you, to hear those words is a very precious thing.

Paul was aware that Tam had a drink problem, but he liked him despite it, and we both felt that the drinking was under control. Tam told Paul he would do anything for me. He even said to Paul, 'If you hurt Dana, I'll kill you.' Paul was actually quite taken with that: he felt Tam was finally accepting some responsibility for me, and was talking like a doting father.

I began to feel more settled around Tam, able to forget that he'd abandoned me and Heather as children and just happy that at last one bit of my own family had come good. I was not exactly proud of him, but I felt good about his presence in our lives. He appeared to have a happy family life of his own, he seemed to adore his own sons, and now he was being a good grandfather to Jordan and an affectionate dad to me and Heather. Affection was something we had never experienced. Mum simply didn't know how to express it.

I even began to think: *This is what we missed out on.* I'd found what I'd been looking for all my life, someone who acted like a parent. Heather quickly started to call him 'Dad', although to me he was always 'Tam'. We even got to know his mother, our grandmother, again. We hadn't seen her since we were little girls, so it felt good to have another piece of my family jigsaw back in place.

Tam was physically affectionate, hugging and kissing us whenever he saw us. I felt slightly uncomfortable with it, but put it down to the fact that as I had not been brought up in a touchy-feely family I wasn't used to people expressing their feelings so openly. There were times, though, when I worried about it, because of my distrust of men in general. I told Paul never to leave me on my own with him. I was never sure whether he was overstepping the mark, or whether I was simply not used to a normal non-sexual relationship with a man, even if he was my father.

I spoke to Tam about Heather, and told him that, because of her history (I only told him the bit about Jamieson), he had to be very careful with her emotions. She was, in some ways, very fragile. In other ways she was more robust than I was, because she was able to shut off her memories. I told him that he should be careful being too physically affectionate with her, as she would probably not know the difference between his affection and the abusive behaviour she had suffered. I said it seriously, but I was not trying to be confrontational: I simply wanted to point out that she needed protecting. For his own sake, too, I told him, 'She sits on your knee because she's just a child inside. But outside she's a grown woman, and it could be misinterpreted. You need to be careful, for your own sake as well as hers. Don't leave yourself open to allegations, make sure there's always someone with you.'

I felt that, as her dad, he needed to understand just how vulnerable she was, and I felt he would want to protect her, like we did.

Then something very serious happened. Paul walked through the hall while Heather was talking on the phone one day. He overheard what she was saying and was immediately worried. She was talking about looking forward to having sex, saying that she would remember to bring the condoms, asking what he would like her to wear, stuff like that. We have always had to be very vigilant about Heather because she's so vulnerable and not able to judge a person's character very well. Even after her experience with Jamieson we've had to stop her from seeing unsuitable boyfriends. It's not that we want to prevent her from having a relationship, it's simply that with her history it would be very easy for any man to take advantage of her.

Paul asked her, 'Who's on the phone, hen?'

'My dad,' she said, unaware that Paul had overheard some of the conversation.

Paul was very alarmed. He didn't confront her there and then about what he'd heard her say. Instead, he told me, and we decided it was likely she used the excuse of talking to her dad to cover up talking to someone else she feared we might not approve of – although Heather is not so devious, and if she does ever tell a lie it is transparent, like a small child's. So we had to be sure, but confronting Heather would not have achieved anything. Instead, Paul fixed the recording device back on to the phone, the one we had used to record Jamieson's threats. Then he rang Tam, had a chat with him, handed the phone over to Heather so that she could talk to him, and walked out of the room so that she would think she was speaking to Tam privately.

I don't know what was said in that conversation. Even to this day, I have refused to listen to the tape that Paul recorded. But I know it shocked and horrified him. It was sexually explicit, and again it hinged around preparations to meet up. Tam had told her he loved her not just as a daughter but as a lover, that she reminded him of Mum, that he didn't class himself as doing anything wrong because he had not been around when she was growing up.

Before we could decide what to do, Tam's partner, whom I liked and got on well with, came to see me. She told me that she was very worried about Tam's relationship with Heather, and that she thought that some of their behaviour was inappropriate. She said that Tam always had Heather on his knee, kissing and cuddling her, and that finally she'd walked in on them in a compromising position.

Paul and I decided to confront Tam. At first he denied everything, said he didn't know what we were talking about, and was very defensive, pretending to be outraged at Paul's accusations. But when Paul told him he had recorded a tape of his phone conversation with Heather, he caved in.

Paul, with his very straightforward, black-and-white morality, said we had to go to the police. I agreed, because Tam had betrayed a serious trust. Not only was Heather his daughter, but she was also, effectively, a child, and so not in any position to make decisions for herself. I found it very hard: not only had he committed a crime against my sister, but I was also devastated to have lost this one bit of normality in my family, the only person who had seemed to behave towards us like a natural parent.

I had to face the fact that I had been deluding myself the whole time. When I basked in the warm glow of finally having a loving father, I had been trying to recreate the fairytale happy family I had never had. I had seen signs pointing to Tam's inappropriate behaviour, but I had always given him the benefit of the doubt because I had invested so much in him: I really, really wanted a good dad for myself and Heather.

Heather was upset when we told her, and didn't really understand why there was anything wrong. But when we explained to her that Tam was her father and it was not right, she was happy to give a statement to the police. Heather is so impressionable, she will do whatever she is asked to do in a situation like the one she found herself in with Tam. After all, she had been groomed for many years to believe that men take advantage of her and that she had to let them do whatever they wanted. It was all she had ever known, from an early age.

I hate Tam for taking advantage of her, and I do feel some guilt for telling him how defenceless she is. She is vulnerable not only because she has learning difficulties, but also because of the life experiences she has had, which meant she agreed to everything he asked her to do.

I think if I had given him the slightest encouragement he would have tried it on with me, too, but I am strong and independent, I'm no longer easily threatened by men, and he realised this. How he thought he would get away with it with Heather, I don't know – or maybe he thought we would turn a blind eye.

A policewoman came to our home to take a statement from Heather. She was kind and gentle with her, and Heather told the whole story. Tam was arrested, charged and pleaded guilty. The judge remanded him on bail for background reports into his living circumstances to be carried out by a social worker. But he disappeared, and didn't turn up when he was supposed to for sentencing. Paul went to court to hear the sentencing, and afterwards he rang a friend who gave him a mobile number which he believed was Tam's. Paul called it and told Tam, 'Listen to me, even if you don't want to say anything. Just listen. Not turning up at court will only mean that you get a longer sentence, and it is only a matter of time until you are caught. I know where you are, and your family will be in trouble for sheltering you. You should do the right thing and apologise to your daughter, and then take the punishment for your crimes.'

We had guessed that he was staying at the house next door to his mother, where his sister's boyfriend lived. Paul was going to tell the police to check it out, but before this could happen Tam turned up at our flat. I was there, with Heather, the children and Mum. I rang Paul and then the police, who came immediately. Tam was very drunk, and he was crying and saying he was sorry. I sent Heather and the children into the bedroom, but Mum sat on the couch, saying nothing. He stood there, pleading with me: 'Dana, can you ever forgive me? Please say you forgive me.'

'No, never,' I said. 'You let me down and you let yourself down. But most of all you took advantage of Heather, when all she needs is love and protection.'

The police took him away and, afterwards, Mum said, 'How could he do that to his own flesh and blood?'

I said nothing, while she and Paul had a long conversation about how low anybody would have to be to touch their own daughter. She said it made her feel sick, and she even went to the toilet and pretended to be sick.

Paul was convinced by her brilliant acting. Later he said to me, 'It's great to see your mum showing some real emotions towards her children, she seemed like a real mother today.'

To me, she overdid it. I know I wanted her to keep up the pretence that she was a normal mum, but this was real hypocrisy. Inwardly I was just wishing she'd let it lie.

For Paul, Tam was the scum of the earth, and I think he felt even more bitter towards him because we had both believed he had turned his life around and was a decent person.

I didn't go to court for the sentencing, but Paul was there to see him get five years.

After his arrest I phoned his mother, my grandmother. She rejected me completely.

'I don't believe my son could ever do anything like that,' she said, and told me she didn't want to see me or Heather ever again. 'I have to support my son,' she said. So we had lost not just a father, but also the rest of his family, again.

Twice since then I have had chance meetings with an aunt and a cousin from that side, and they have both blanked me. I know they recognised me, but they chose to ignore me. I can live with that, although each time it has caused me a moment's sadness. I never harmed them, I'm not the guilty one.

Tam's out of prison now, and we've had no contact with him, neither have we seen him around. I do keep in touch with his ex-partner and his three sons, and we see them now and again. She understands the situation, and she doesn't have any resentment towards us for calling the police. She had her own suspicions about him, and she is glad that in the end he was brought to justice. She copes very well on her own with her family.

I feel no guilt or regret about what happened to my father; I hate him for betraying my trust. It took me a long time, living with Paul and learning that not everybody in the world is out to take advantage of me, for me to begin to be less suspicious of everyone I met. Tam's behaviour set me back a bit. He didn't completely destroy the progress I had made, but because of him, once again, I was very wary of allowing myself to trust and love someone.

Writing this book, I have found it much harder to recall the abuse that Heather suffered than anything that happened to me. I can hardly bear to think of the things that were done to her. She is so trusting, so vulnerable. It is hard to accept that my own father – *her* own father – was just another of the pack. He is yet another abnormal man my mother drew into her life – one who, worst of all, shares our blood. As far as I'm concerned, I no longer have a father. That dream is dead to me. Now there's another question that haunts my thoughts, *How could he?*

9

It was soon after Jordan was born that another drama ripped our lives apart and, once again, made me wonder, *How could she?* How could my mother have behaved the way she did?

I had taken Jordan shopping, leaving Heather alone at home. We were still very worried about Jamieson, although the threats had stopped and everything seemed calmer. We continued to take a great deal of care with her, chauffeuring her around if she went to visit friends, and making sure she locked the door when she was at home.

When I got back with the shopping she wasn't there. I didn't panic immediately, but I rang Paul, and he came back as soon as he could. It was only then that I realised some of her clothes were also gone, and a cold fear gripped me. There was no sign of her having been taken against her will, but my imagination raced to the worst conclusions.

Paul had to calm me down, and we agreed to drive around to a friend of Heather's to see if she was there.

She wasn't, but the friend was able to tell us what had happened. Heather had been taken away by Alan, Mum's boyfriend. It was such a shock that I had to sit down while I struggled to take it in. Paul's reaction was immediate: he was furious.

Heather's friend told us that Alan was taking her to Arbroath, by coincidence the same place that Jamieson had taken her. Alan had family there. It was hard to believe: we had our reservations about Alan but, as far as we knew, he seemed to have a good relationship with Mum and to be looking after her, and we had certainly never seen him taking any special interest in Heather. However, he had apparently been worried that Rab was about to be released from jail, and had thought Mum might go back to him.

As soon as he heard the news, Paul rang Alan's mobile.

'Get back down here with her now, this minute, or I'm coming to get her – and you'll be sorry,' he said, probably with a few expletives thrown in. Paul is a big, forceful character, and his tirade was enough to stop Alan, literally, in his tracks.

Alan drove back to our flat with Heather straightaway, fortunately without having had time to take advantage of her. Paul told Alan exactly what he thought of him. Alan apologised and pathetically tried to justify himself. He would not leave our flat even after I asked him to go. Mum was there too. She did not seem at all upset about what had happened, and even appeared to be defending Alan.

I shouldn't have been so surprised by this given her past actions when men were involved.

I said to her, 'If you go back with him; I'll never speak to you again. You have a choice. Either you choose him, or you choose Heather and me.'

She didn't even think about it for more than a few seconds.

'I choose Alan,' she said.

That summed everything up, completely. Given a choice she would always put her man of the moment before her daughters, even a man who had run away with one of them. There was no pressure on her; Alan was not the sort of man who could have frightened her into staying with him. So she didn't even have that excuse. It wasn't as though he was even a great catch. Any normal person would have made the choice just as quickly, but with the opposite result. She should have picked her children. She should have said to him, 'It's wrong what you did to my daughter and I'm standing by my kids.'

She had a chance to start making up, in a small way, for what she had done to us. But she didn't take the chance. She'd betrayed us, yet again. I remember looking at her and thinking, *This is what you have done all your life. Whenever you had the opportunity to be a good mum, you turned your back on it, and you turned your back on us, me and Heather.*

Because it came so soon after Jordan's birth, those hours when she sat by my side in the hospital, pretending to be a loving, caring mother, this new betrayal hurt deeply, even though I should have expected it.

Even after Mum said she would stick by him, Alan still wouldn't leave our flat: he was going on and on and on, trying to defend himself, so that in the end we had to call the police to have him removed. The police said that if Heather had gone with him willingly there was nothing they could do, as she was an adult and nothing untoward had happened, despite the fact that she had the mental age of a child. But they made sure he left our home. Mum went with him.

Before he ran away with Heather, Alan sold all his expensive electronic equipment, including his plasma-screen television, his hi-fi and his computer keyboard and screen. He got a few hundred pounds for it all, even though it was worth thousands. Paul was with him when he sold it all, and had quizzed Alan as to why he was getting rid of his valuable possessions – Alan simply said he needed the money. When they were in the shop completing the sale, Alan suddenly changed his mind and retrieved the computer tower, the part that houses the hard drive. It seemed suspicious to Paul, who instantly wondered what was on the hard drive that Alan did not want others to see.

Paul later told the police about the computer tower, which, according to Heather, Alan had taken to Arbroath with him. When the police questioned him about it he caved in and admitted that it was full of child pornography. The police seized it from his daughter's home in Arbroath, and when they checked out its contents there were lots of images of children being horrifically abused. Alan was actually in the shop trying to buy back his electrical goods when he was arrested.

Mum has always said she didn't know about the child pornography, but it seems to me that she must have done. The computer had been next to the bed in their bedroom, she must have known it was there. And from the quantity of material downloaded on it, she must have been aware of him spending a lot of time online. It seems unlikely that she had no idea what he was doing, especially as a lot of the material was downloaded while he was away doing his driving job. She claimed to be shocked and disgusted by it, but why would she be shocked and disgusted by images on a screen, when she had been part of similar acts herself?

I have always wondered if she told Alan what had happened to me and Heather. Was that why he felt it would be easy to run off with Heather? I hate the idea of him getting kicks out of hearing about my abuse. It makes me feel as though I have been abused all over again.

People talk about the downloading of child pornography as if it is a lesser crime than actually abusing children, but nobody should ever forget that, for every image of a child being raped or molested that appears on the computer screen, somewhere a child was abused in real life in order to provide the film or the image. The men who look at child pornography *are* abusers, they are providing a market for this terrible material, and to feed that market children are suffering.

I believe that looking at child pornography makes it easier to become an abuser in real life. For some individuals, seeing other people abusing children validates it, makes it seem both possible and acceptable. Alan himself admitted this later to Paul when he said that he felt his urges getting stronger.

After he was arrested he was released on bail, but this time Mum did not take him back, and he was homeless. For a time he lodged at the house of an Irishman, who had no idea about the crime Alan was on bail for, and who occasionally left Alan at home with his children. When the Irishman discovered what Alan was charged with, he went mad, and Alan had to go into hiding. The Irishman would probably have done real damage to him if he had found him.

At this point Alan started ringing Paul, threatening to shoot him. He said he had a gun. We found out later that he had tried to get a gun from the Irishman. Paul informed the police, and they arranged to tape record Alan's calls to our house. They traced a call he made from a phone box at our local Asda, and although he didn't know it, an armed response car tailed him as he left the supermarket car park and drove away. After a few hundred yards the police pulled his car over and he was arrested at gunpoint. They searched the car and there was no gun. He was charged with making threats to kill, and given bail.

Within hours of being released, he went to Wester Hailes police station and told the duty officer that he was going to go after Paul unless they arrested him. I think he wanted to be held in custody, as that was the only way he could be safe from the anger of the Irishman, who was actively looking for him, and who frightened him far more than the prospect of being held in a police cell. The police didn't take him seriously, so within minutes of leaving the police station he turned up outside our flat and tried to throw a boulder through our window. We live on the second floor, and he could not throw it high enough. But he was clearly caught on CCTV camera doing it. We called the police, and he waited there for them to come. This time they took him into custody.

'That's great,' he told them, 'That's what I want.' He was clearly relieved to be locked up.

I'm not sure what the final charges were when his trial came up, but he pleaded guilty and served a short prison sentence.

Mum, in the meantime, wasted no time in finding another boyfriend, and moving in with him. (I won't name him, because he was not a paedophile and he suffered a great shock when the truth about Mum came out. He practically had a full-scale breakdown at the thought that he had been so close to her.) Granddad moved in with them both, because he was lonely living on his own, and it was while Mum's boyfriend was away visiting a sick relative that another young child, only three years old, may have had a lucky escape. The mother arranged for her daughter to be looked after by Mum, and to stay the night there. Mum said the little girl could have Granddad's bed and Granddad would sleep on the settee. But when the mother took her little girl's bag through to the bedroom she realised the settee was in the same room, and she changed her mind sharply. She really let rip at Mum and Granddad, and left their flat screaming abuse, calling them 'perverts'. This was before anything was known about either of them, but her instincts were right.

When I heard about the incident later, I waited until I was on my own with Mum. Then I really laid into her.

'How could you even think about babysitting? How could you let him near anyone else's children? Don't you think enough damage has been done?'

As usual, she was unmoved.

'I didn't think,' was all she said.

It was not the first time that Mum had volunteered to babysit: I'd found her looking after children before, and quietly warned her off. I'm not sure whether she and Granddad would have done anything that night, because of the risk of being caught. But they'd given in to temptation and taken risks before, so I can't be sure. All I do know is that neither of them should ever have been left in charge of children, and I'm just glad for that little girl that she didn't spend the night there.

Heather repeated the allegations against Granddad after Alan's and then Tam's arrests. It was as if her treatment by Jamieson and then by Alan and our dad, and the fuss everyone made about the way they treated her, triggered her memories of the abuse she suffered from Granddad.

This time Paul mentioned her accusations against Granddad when Auntie Brenda was at our house. Brenda, as Granddad's other daughter, was outraged, and she insisted on ringing the police. I was more frightened than ever: it was all going to come out. The whole can of worms would be opened, and the full scale of the abuse would be laid bare.

I remember lying awake in bed, listening to Paul's regular breathing as he slept, feeling the bulk of him next to me, and wondering if this was all the happiness God was going to allow me. Something inside me still believed that I didn't deserve happiness. I had been told so often and for so long by Granddad and Nana King that I was worthless, and even though I rejected everything they said, at some deep level I still felt this new, happy life wouldn't be mine for long, because with a history like mine I just didn't deserve it. I knew, rationally, that I had been a small child and was horribly betrayed by the adults around me, but I still felt what they had done to me made me unlovable. All I could think about was that I loved Paul, and I wanted to keep him, and if he knew the truth about me he would not stay.

Paul still had no idea about Granddad's involvement with me. He knew how easy it was to make Heather out as a liar, because it was easy to confuse her, but this time he believed everything Heather said.

'She keeps saying it. She's not making it up – why would she? She's telling the truth. However good he was to you as a grandfather, he was abusing Heather, I'm sure of it,' he told me.

I just agreed with him, but in my heart I felt sick.

Before the police had time to interview Granddad, we met him at the house Mum was now living at with her latest boyfriend. We didn't go there to see Granddad, but as soon as I realised he was there I knew Paul would confront him. Paul is so straightforward: if something is wrong, he wants to put it right, to sort it out as soon as possible.

Mum was busy in the kitchen, out of earshot, when Paul broached the subject. He chose the moment deliberately, because he naturally assumed it would be very difficult for her to hear that her own father had been molesting her daughter.

Paul told Granddad that the police had been called in, and that they were interviewing Jamieson as well. He caved in and admitted it straightaway. Mum walked back into the room and when she realised what he was saying she was very angry with him – but, not, astonishingly, for what he had done, but for owning up to it.

She said to him, 'There's no evidence – it's your word against Heather's. You shouldn't have admitted it in front of witnesses.'

Paul later told me he was gobsmacked by how cold Mum was, and he was horrified that she sprang so quickly to Granddad's defence and didn't seem to care about what he had done to her daughter.

'It's all out now. What's done is done,' was all Granddad managed to say. He seemed resigned to it. He told Mum that Jamieson was going to be a witness against him.

But Mum just exclaimed, 'If you admit the fucking crime, you'll do the fucking time.' She was adamant that he should retract what he had said, and kept telling him he hadn't admitted anything in front of the police, and he shouldn't.

Paul interrupted her to remind Granddad that he had confessed in front of witnesses, including Mum's boyfriend, one of the few decent men she was ever involved with.

Granddad didn't apologise for what he had done, and talked about raping Heather in a very matter-of-fact way. I was aware of him glancing slyly at me, checking whether or not I was involved in the allegations against him. When he saw that I wasn't, he never mentioned abusing me, and I was glad of that. The police came, arrested him, and took statements from those of us who had witnessed his confession. Mum claimed she had not heard it. Later they interviewed Heather and me, and while Heather told the truth, I kept up my pretence.

'He was a good grandfather to me, he never bothered me,' I said.

It wasn't that I was in denial; I knew perfectly well what he had done. I wasn't blocking the memory, I just wanted to keep myself clear of all the allegations. I was scared that once I told the truth about Granddad's abuse, I might not be able to stop myself letting all the rest of it come tumbling out. It would be like turning on a tap and not being able to turn it off again. The very thought that Paul might learn about all the dirty men who had forced themselves on me made me shudder. I wanted everything to carry on as it had been, and was even more determined to push it to the back of my mind and carry on with my life.

It seemed to me that Paul must already be wondering

what kind of family I came from, what with Alan, Jamieson, Tam, and now Granddad, convicted or accused of taking advantage of my sister.

Paul was very tuned in to my moods, and he quietly persisted in asking me about Granddad.

One night, as we were sitting on our bed talking, I finally said to him, 'You keep asking me about Granddad. I've got something to tell you.'

I admitted to him everything that Granddad had done to me. I sat rigid on the bed, not looking at him, with my eyes focussing on the floor a few feet in front of me. I was convinced he wouldn't love me any more, and that once he knew it would all be over between us. But I couldn't keep on lying. I could keep things hidden – I didn't at this stage tell him anything about all the other abuse – but I couldn't lie when he asked me direct questions. He had no clue about anything else, and it was only Granddad he asked me about.

Paul was not shocked: he had suspected all along that I had also been abused, which is why he'd been gently trying to get me to open up about everything. The police were taking Heather very seriously, and Paul felt sure I was also involved. He knew me well enough to feel my denials did not ring true. It also seemed logical that we would both have been victims.

Paul is by nature talkative, but he sat in silence until I had finished, and then he wrapped his arms around me and held me close, stroking my hair and reassuring me that he still loved me, and that everything would be all right. I cried in his arms, relieved that this ordeal was over, but

I felt that something more dreadful was to come. If the truth about Granddad was out, how long would it be before the rest was uncovered?

At that moment I couldn't face Paul knowing any of the other stuff. Granddad had been the least of my abusers, the easiest one to deal with, both physically and emotionally. I'm not running away from the fact that what he did to me was appalling, and would be considered a very serious crime in any civilised society, but for me, as a child whose perspective on right and wrong was so distorted by the appallingly cruel, sadistic and deviant behaviour of the others, Granddad's abuse was both short-lived and predictable. It is, I can see now, a measure of how awful the rest of my childhood had been, that I regarded Granddad's perverted behaviour as lightweight.

After Granddad's arrest, he was released on bail. He went to live in a hostel, because Mum's boyfriend refused to allow him to live with them. However, he was so horrified that she continued to support Granddad that he eventually split up with her.

I was finding it harder and harder to cope. For the sake of the children, Paul, and all my future happiness, I was still suppressing thoughts about my childhood, still keeping up the pretence that the only abuse I ever suffered was from Granddad. I became difficult and tetchy; short-tempered with Paul, and not as patient as I should have been with the children. Every day was a struggle, and every night I found it hard to sleep, haunted by dreams in which I was back in the House of Hell.

Paul was kind and gentle with me: he thought it was all the result of my difficulty coping with what had happened to Heather. It's true, I was feeling an enormous amount of guilt about her. It was as though I had created the situation which allowed her to be abused when I stopped going to my grandparents' house. I had hideous moments when I dwelled upon it: if I had continued to go there, and let Granddad abuse me, would that have saved Heather? Should I have been more aware at the time what was happening to her? I was only eight when Granddad started abusing her, but I felt I should have helped her more.

Behind my dark moods was the ever-present fear that the whole truth would now come out, and I would lose everything. I suppose I should have realised, from the way Paul reacted to the news that Granddad had abused me, that he was a strong man with a deep love for me. But could any love be deep enough to take in the awful things that had happened at the House of Hell and in Abernethy? I really didn't think so. All I wanted was to be able to control my life, not let these awful memories keep creeping in.

What happened next was beyond my control. It was an innocent enough event, but it unleashed in me a terror so great that I was convinced life was no longer worth living.

10

The man at the door was smartly dressed, and wearing a dark suit and tie. It was a dark winter's evening, but I could clearly see him in the light from the open front door, and I recognised him immediately. He was Denver Petch, whose half-brother Mo had abused me for so long when I was a child. Denver Petch had never been involved in the abuse; he had done nothing to me, and he had no idea what his brother had done. He was entirely innocent. But he was related to Mo, and that was enough to convulse me with loathing and fear. It was like a very unpleasant and physical blast from the past that finally pushed me beyond my limit.

'Hello, Dana, are you all right, hen?' he asked. He was friendly, smiling at me, greeting me normally. I knew why he was on my doorstep: he had come to collect our £10 instalment on a loan we were paying back to a loan company. It wasn't a big loan – we'd needed money for some furniture.

It was the arrest of Tam that brought him to my doorstep. Until then, we had paid for the loan at Tam's house, to the same collector who called for Tam's money. After his arrest, I'd phoned the finance company and arranged for them to come to our address. This was the first visit. I had no idea, until I opened the door to him, that it would be one of the Petch family.

I had the money ready and I handed it to him without speaking, as if I was on autopilot. Heather and the children were in the house, but Paul was out. I went back inside, and tried to carry on as if nothing had happened. I had dinner to make and Jordan to bath. But I needed time to think, and the only place I could go to for privacy was the toilet. I locked myself in, sat down, and put my head in my hands. I felt a rising tide of panic, as though my past was being swept towards me and would engulf me, drag me under and never let me surface.

I could no longer control or suppress it. That day, I knew with complete certainty, that I couldn't carry on with my double life. I hated everything that had happened to me, and that made me hate myself. I had been strong for years, but I just felt I didn't have the strength to carry on any more. I had Paul, Jordan, Ryan, Young Paul and Heather, all relying on me to keep myself together, to be the anchor for the whole family. I couldn't do it any longer. I couldn't keep putting other people's needs first. I wanted to get away from it all, from the terrible thoughts that were swarming through my brain. From the memories. From the feeling of worthlessness. From myself.

I went into the living room and looked at the children. They were glued to a cartoon on the television, and Ryan was laughing delightedly at the antics of the characters. I felt sick as I looked at them, feeling that I was going to betray all their happiness as well as my own if I let the past catch up with me. Part of me wanted to stand on the rooftops and scream to the world all the details of the abuse, to make ordinary people aware of the terrible things that some children have to suffer. I wanted the string of paedophiles who had raped me off the streets, so that my sons would be safe. But another, louder, part of me wanted it all to go away, to just come to a quick end, because I was terrified of losing the family we'd become. I felt everything would disintegrate, Paul would not stand by me, and Jordan and I would be on our own in life.

Like a robot I somehow managed to finish the housework and get the kids into bed. When Paul came home I said nothing to him about Denver Petch, and I tried to chat about normal, everyday things. But as the evening wore on, it became more and more of a struggle for me to think about anything else.

I felt dirty, I felt horrible. I felt that all the work I had done for the past nine years, building up this picture of myself as normal, had been undone. If I told Paul, he would not only have to come to terms with what had happened to me, but also with the fact that I had lied and lied and lied to him. It was all over, I was sure of it.

At about ten o'clock I went through to the bedroom, telling Paul I wanted an early night. As I closed the door behind me I felt my legs give way under me and I slumped to the floor, sobbing. After a while I picked myself up and sat on the edge of the bed. There was a full bottle of insulin in my handbag, enough to last nearly two weeks. It was my way out: I could inject myself with the whole bottle, and it would all be over. I could go to a safe place, a place where nobody would ever know my dirty secrets. If I died, my family would be distraught, but they need never know the shameful truth about me. It would be easier for all of them if I wasn't here.

I justified it all in my mind. Paul was a good and loving dad, who could take care of Jordan as well as the other two boys. If they knew the truth about me, none of them would want me, not just Paul but the kids too. How could anyone love and want a woman as their mother or wife when she had been so contaminated? My self-esteem was rock-bottom.

As I slid the needle into my arm, all I wanted was oblivion. Maybe there was a God, a Heaven, a place where all the sins that had been committed against me would be washed away. I felt sure that could not happen on this earth. And if there was no Heaven, well, at least I would escape the ever-increasing daily torment of my past that made the future seem so impossible, so bleak. I wanted to be free of the worry, free of the constant battle to be strong and positive.

When Paul came to bed he tried to move me, as I was

sprawled right across it. When I didn't respond, he began to panic. He knew I was not asleep because I was so deeply out of it. Putting the light on, he saw the empty bottle of insulin and the syringe, and he realised what I had done. He dialled 999, and within minutes an ambulance was there.

I have no memory of what happened: all I know is that I woke up in hospital with a doctor shouting, 'Can you hear me?'

He had a massive syringe in his hand, and he was rigging up a drip into my arm.

Apparently, Paul was told that I might not pull through. I had been in a deep coma and my blood sugars had dropped alarmingly. As I came round I saw Paul's worried face, and it took me a few moments to remember what I had done. I instantly regretted it: the look on Paul's face told me how badly it had shocked and hurt him, and I realised that everyone else around me would feel the same. I had only succeeded in making the man I loved feel wretched and as though he had failed me, which was the last thing I wanted. At the same time, my big problem had not been solved.

After a while I drifted off to sleep again. When I opened my eyes Paul was at my bedside, holding my hand. He smiled at me, and I was overcome by a huge rush of love for him. How could I have thought that escaping my demons was worth losing this, the only real love I had ever known? I tried to speak, but he shushed me, and stroked my hair.

'I know something's seriously bothering you, Dana,' he said. I struggled to speak but he put his finger gently over my lips. 'No, don't say anything. Just rest. But I want you to know that whatever it is, you can tell me. I love you, Dana. You are the best thing that has ever happened to me; I want to be with you for the rest of my life. I couldn't bear it if anything happened to you.'

I drifted off to sleep again, and when I woke he was still there. I knew I had to tell him something. When your partner attempts suicide, it must feel like a terrible betrayal, as if I was telling him that no matter how much I loved him and the children, it was not enough to stop me wanting to die. He knew there was something seriously wrong, but he didn't have a clue what it was. At first he was actually worried that I had been having an affair and that I was too afraid to tell him. If only it had been that simple.

I knew I owed him an explanation, but I was too weak and tired to cope with it while I was on a hospital ward. I was in hospital for two days, and because I had attempted suicide a psychiatrist also had to visit me. I told him I had been very stupid, and that I wouldn't do it again. He seemed satisfied, and I didn't have to go into any detail as to why I'd tried to kill myself. I think he believed – and I half felt it myself – that I'd taken the overdose simply to give myself a long sleep, without any thought about the real danger of death.

Once I was home, Paul's questions became more insistent. He really needed to know why I had done it, so I finally found enough courage to tell him that I had been abused, just once, by Morris Petch. I told him that the sight of Denver Petch on my doorstep had brought it flooding back. We had been sitting on the edge of the bed again, talking late into the night, and when Paul heard my explanation he jumped up. At first, for one dreadful moment, I felt he was moving to get away from me.

In fact, he was consumed with anger towards Morris Petch. It's a good thing we had no idea where he was living, because I think that in his blind rage Paul would have gone out to kill him there and then. As soon as that violent emotion subsided, he sat down again and pulled me against his chest. I don't think he has ever realised how reassuring that small gesture was to me. He didn't shudder with disgust at the thought of this dirty man forcing himself on me. Instead, he hugged me and comforted me.

'It's you I love. I hate him for what he did to you, but I don't hate you. You were a child. If anything, Dana, I love you even more because of what you have been through,' he said. It felt so good to hear him say those words, and I remember sinking back into my pillow with a feeling of contentment that I had not known since Heather first raised the subject of Granddad's abuse. The nervousness and insecurity that had gnawed at me began to seep away.

I felt better, but painfully aware that what I had told Paul was only the tip of the iceberg. We didn't discuss going to the police about Morris Petch, probably because Paul thought it had only happened once, and I certainly wasn't ready to do any more than tell Paul. At that time, the idea that the whole world would one day find out the truth about Heather's and my childhood would have horrified me. But I had come to the conclusion in hospital that I couldn't avoid my past for the rest of my life.

Jordan, who was eight months old, was delighted to see me when I got home from hospital. It was as he stretched his arms out to be picked up and hugged, that I finally made the decision to tell the truth. It suddenly hit me that some of my abusers were still out there, possibly still abusing other small, frightened children. Some were dead, but some were still very much alive. I looked at my own baby boy and was filled with horror at the idea that he could ever be a victim, that anyone could even think about treating him in the way Heather and I had been treated.

I resolved to tell Paul the whole story, bar the truth about my mum's involvement. I made up my mind to tell him all about the Kings, Morris Petch and John O'Flaherty. But I couldn't and wouldn't tell him about what my mum had done. I was convinced that was too much to expect anyone to believe. I swore to myself I was *never* going to bring her into it.

As I'd grown up, created my own family, got to know more and more people, I increasingly realised that my mother's behaviour flew in the face of everything we all know and hold dear about motherhood. Her betrayal remains the most terrible thing that happened to me, far worse than anything physical that she or the others did to me. It was that total sense of helplessness, having nobody in the world to turn to, that dominated my childhood, and she alone was responsible for that. However, I couldn't completely throw away the make-believe happy family I had so carefully constructed over so many years.

My mother's crimes were too dark for any outsider to comprehend. The lie we shared was better for everyone.

Before I had a chance to confess it all to Paul, we were swallowed up by another drama. Two days after I got home, Heather took an insulin overdose too. She was not unconscious, and I don't think she realised the gravity of what she had done. She just came to me one day and said, 'I've taken my whole bottle of insulin.'

I took one look at her and realised she was telling the truth. Paul phoned for an ambulance, and she was rushed to hospital. I travelled with her, going back to where I had been only two days earlier myself. I stayed with her as late as I could, because Heather finds it difficult to cope with unfamiliar surroundings. Then I went back the next day, and again stayed with her for as long as possible, leaving Paul to cope at home. They kept her in for a couple of days.

I don't want to play down or underestimate Heather's suffering in any way: I think she has had a terrible life, worse than mine in many ways. But I'm not sure that she was trying to kill herself. She is very influenced by me, and when she saw all the attention I got after my suicide attempt, I think she wanted her share of the fuss. Heather lives for each day; she doesn't dwell on the past or the future, as I do. I see my job as her carer to keep each day as happy as it can be: if Heather is happy in the present, that's what matters.

When I got home Paul talked to me very sternly.

'Heather copies you, even down to what mood she is in. It's very dangerous for her to see you attempting to kill yourself, because she just copies. The children, too, are very impressionable. How are they going to cope if they think that the way you deal with problems is by taking an overdose?'

I could see the sense in what he was saying. Of course, he had no idea of the extent of my inner turmoil and might not have said this had he known, but his words rang true. He was right that I was acting irresponsibly towards the children and Heather.

In the end, I didn't sit down with Paul and explain everything in full as I had planned. All I could bear to do was tell him gradually, bit by bit, over a few weeks. I'd tell him something and then stop myself in case I had said too much. I still felt there was an invisible barrier that, when I crossed it, would mean I would never be able to get back to the warmth and security of his love. No matter how many times he told me that nothing I could possibly tell him would stop him loving me, I was wary. I constantly looked for signs that he was physically repulsed by me. I was always anxious that he would find what I was telling him too distasteful to contemplate. But Paul seemed to be able to absorb and deal with it all.

Years later, when it all came out in public, when people actually asked him, 'How do you feel about all those dirty old men touching and having sex with your partner?' He would simply reply, 'They didn't touch or have sex with the woman I love. They touched a poor, defenceless little girl who couldn't stop them. I love her even more for the child she once was.'

I'm not saying that it was an easy time for us. We spent endless hours, deep into the darkest time of the night, talking it through, me slowly adding little pieces of the story to what he already knew. He was very, very angry, and incredibly hurt on my behalf. He was also in shock that the person he had been so close to, and who he thought he knew so well, could have been hiding something so immense from him. He was loving and supportive, but also shattered by the enormity of it all. He had a great deal of anger to cope with: his instinct, like that of most men, I think, was to go round and personally deal with Morris Petch and John O'Flaherty and any of the others I named who were not already dead. He wanted to kill anyone who had hurt me, to make them suffer too, but we both realised that this was not the way forward.

Perhaps the hardest thing for him to come to terms with at this stage was his assessment of Billy. He'd been sure that Billy had been a good, generous and caring father figure to me. He'd cleaned up Billy's grave as a present to me. He'd taken Jordan as a baby to the grave, to introduce him to the step-granddad he would never know, but who had been such an important person in his mother's life. Paul had, without ever meeting him, taken a real liking to Billy. And all because I was a good and convincing actress. Now, he had to revise his opinions, but he also had to come to terms with the fact that I had concealed so much from him. I felt desperately guilty about misleading him, even though he reassured me that he could understand why I had done so. But I think it really did hurt him deeply that I had not been able to trust him with my secrets, and for that reason I regret it.

Our relationship was under great stress. Neither of us was sleeping much, and for me it was all terrifying. Although Paul had not turned his back on me, which had been my worst fear, another of my fears had come to pass: the normality of our lives seemed to be over. The world I had created was gone. Instead of talking about Jordan's first teeth, what Ryan was doing at school, what we were going to eat that evening, suddenly our only topic of conversation was my childhood abuse. It had come centre stage again, and I hated it.

I often thought: why did I do this? Why could I not let the past lie?

Paul found his own way of coping. He was so outraged to discover that paedophiles could operate and flourish in Edinburgh, the city he had known and loved since he was a child, that he began to speak out publicly on the subject. He rang a radio talk show and found himself on air, telling all the listeners that keeping paedophilia behind closed doors was a recipe for disaster, and that the only way forward was to shine a light into the dark places where paedophiles lurked.

Of course, he couldn't mention that his own partner was a victim, because this could have prejudiced any future legal action, and because I certainly was not ready to be identified. But he spoke in general terms. Paul is a forceful and fluent speaker, and there was a great and very supportive response from other radio listeners. The talk-show host, Mike Graham of Talk 107, was happy to host more call-in programmes on the topic, as it had so obviously hit a public nerve.

Within weeks, Paul had enough people wanting to join him in his crusade that he set up the Society Against Paedophiles, which at its height had several hundred supporters. I was never involved and, to be honest, I didn't want Paul to get in so deep: I was still coming to terms with admitting what had happened to me, I wasn't ready to worry about other victims or to take part in any campaigns. I had to accept that it was his way of coping, however, and he needed to channel his anger and hatred in some way. He knew he couldn't change what had happened to me, but he wanted to help other children who were currently being abused, or who were at risk from paedophiles.

In those early days I neither approved nor disapproved of what Paul was doing. I understood how hard my revelations had hit him, and when he said he was setting up the society for me, I didn't want to discourage him, particularly as so many people seemed to feel the same way he did.

The Society Against Paedophiles was a loose collaboration of like-minded individuals. They networked, and when they had information about the whereabouts of known paedophiles, they let the local community know.

Paul set up a website and on it he explained: 'We are not

a vigilante group, we are law-abiding citizens who feel the need to protect Scotland's most vulnerable, while the Government plays catch-up with reality.'

The support he got was amazing: victims and other individuals even donated cars; a local company tinted the windows of the cars and had the name of the society printed on to them; other companies provided free cleaning, repair and fuelling of the vehicles.

Of course, the very existence of the organisation was controversial. Understandably, the police didn't like the attention Paul's group created by driving around in cars with blacked-out windows and the words Society Against Paedophiles printed on the sides.

Paul was accused of becoming 'a fanatic' in his crusade against paedophiles. Today he argues, 'Who wouldn't be a fanatic if their partner had been raped over and over again by paedophiles? I only have to think of the image of Dana, a young scared child, huddled in her bed, waiting to be raped, for my blood to boil. I felt so much sympathy and sadness for her – but I also felt anger.

'Although I can never claim that I have been affected anywhere near as much as she has, I – and all the other family members – are the hidden victims. Everyone around Dana, everyone who loves her, is in some way affected – and the same goes for all victims of paedophiles. They don't just damage the child, they damage all those involved in that child's life. The net is spread very wide.'

Their campaign was along the lines of the Sarah's Law campaign in England. After the murder of eight-year-old

Sarah Payne by paedophile Roy Whiting there was a massive groundswell of opinion in favour of publicising the whereabouts of known paedophiles who posed a threat to children. The campaign has resulted in fourteen new pieces of legislation which give greater powers to employers so that they are able to check the backgrounds of anyone working with children, even though it has not resulted in its original aim to give all parents the legal right to know the identity of serious child sex offenders living in their community.

In Scotland, attempts to get a Sarah's Law on to the statute books were turned down because of the risk of driving sex offenders underground. Paul believed this was a risk worth taking, and that his Society Against Paedophiles could help make sure there was no hiding place for any of them. Given that I'm a mother myself, I agree with him that no parent should ever have to worry about their children being at risk from the man next door, or the man down the street. But in my case it was the parent who'd betrayed me, who'd willingly offered me to the man down the street, and unknown to Paul I was still trying to come to terms with this. At the time I also strongly felt that I didn't want the light shone on my mum.

I continued to have no interest in joining Paul's society or getting involved with what he was doing, though I supported his views and felt as outraged as he did about the lack of support for victims. I could relate to it: society *should* be against paedophiles.

But, however much I applauded his motives and the

aims of his society, I found Paul's involvement with it very unsettling. It took up so much of his time, taking him away from his family, and, worst of all, it meant that all our conversations centred around paedophiles and sexual abuse. I was emotionally exhausted by my own problems, and there seemed to be no relief from them.

11

Angela Edmunds is another heroine of my story. She's a detective constable, working in the Family Protection Unit, the unit that deals with domestic violence and child abuse – the crimes that happen behind the closed doors of seemingly respectable families. She'd seen and heard a lot before she met me and Heather, but she admits that what she uncovered in our family was far worse and far more widespread than anything she had come across before.

To me, she is a saviour. She has always been there for me, always been willing to listen to me, always had time to give me advice and comfort. I can text her or phone her at any time, and she'll get back to me as soon as she can. Without her, I'm not sure that I would have had the courage to pursue justice in the way that I have done. She made a very difficult business a lot easier, because of her personality and her dedication to her job.

It took me a while to feel completely comfortable with her, to be able to open up to her. I think if it had been any other police officer, I might never have been able to speak so freely. But Angela didn't come across like a person in authority, a detective constable. I didn't feel she looked down on me and although she was always kind, she didn't make me feel that she pitied me. I hate pity; I don't want people to feel sorry for me. Angela was great. She has a couple of kids herself, so she understood what it was like for me having to carry on with normal family life while going through all the police interviews, and she was always happy to work around my other commitments.

At first, I was very embarrassed talking about the physical details of what happened to me. But Angela was not prim and proper, she said it was all right for me to swear if I wanted to, and she made me feel comfortable using the anatomical language necessary to be precise about the abuse. Even when I wasn't doing interviews with her, she always kept in touch. She'd text me in the evenings, just to see that I was OK.

I had met her already: she was the police officer handling the investigation into Granddad. She had interviewed Heather about the abuse she'd suffered from him, and I had seen how gentle and kind she was with her. (At that stage, I was still insisting that Granddad had not touched me.) So when Paul and I agreed that we had to do something about my abusers, he rang her. He didn't have to persuade me: I knew that the only right thing to do was to tell the police now that it was all coming out. My head was all over the place, but the one thing I was clear about was that these men should not be walking the streets. I wanted them to go to jail for what they had done.

When Paul rang Angela all he said was, 'Dana's been telling me about being abused as a child, and I think you should hear what she has to say.'

It was a couple of days later that Angela arrived at our flat, on her own. Initially it was very hard to talk. It had been difficult telling Paul; it was far worse telling someone who was practically a stranger. At that first meeting we covered just the bare outline of what I wanted to tell her.

After that she made an appointment for me to go to St Leonard's Police Station, where the Family Protection Unit is based. I was interviewed there in informal surroundings: they have a comfortable room, with sofas and a coffee table, and with tea and coffee and soft drinks available. It doesn't exactly feel like home, but it's the nearest thing and feels far less cold and intimidating than a regular interview room.

Over the next few meetings I grew to feel much more comfortable talking to Angela, and I spent so many hours there that that room became almost a second home to me. Eventually, I told her everything.

Well, once again, not quite everything. I still couldn't tell her, or Paul, about Mum's involvement. I told Angela about Billy and Granddad King, about John O'Flaherty and Morris Petch, and about the men who raped me at Abernethy, whose identities I didn't know. But I always made it sound as though Billy orchestrated it all and Mum knew nothing about it. I was protecting her, but also protecting myself from the terrible truth, that even my own mother had abused me.

The other people I didn't initially tell her about were Nana King and Mum's father, Granddad, even though I'd told Paul about him. Why did I hold back about Nana King? I didn't owe that sadistic old lady any loyalty, and she had been dead for ten years by this time. I think, with hindsight, that I held back because she was another woman, and by admitting she took part, I opened up the possibility that Mum had also been involved. While I kept it to a collection of dirty old men, Mum's involvement wasn't questioned, whereas if I involved Nana King, it made it possible to believe any woman from my childhood could do it.

As for not telling about Granddad, that, too, was to keep the whole shame and disgust as far away from association with my immediate family as possible, even though the police knew what he had done to Heather – and I'm sure Angela must have suspected that he'd abused me, too.

All in all, I had about fifteen interviews with Angela, each time going into more and more detail about the terrible things that had happened to me. By the end, I'd told her about Nana King and, eventually, much later, about Granddad. She talked to Heather as well. Strangely, Heather and I never discussed what we said to Angela, just as we had, for so many years, never discussed the abuse we'd shared. I had no idea what Heather was telling her, but I know now that Heather corroborated everything about Granddad and Nana King, and about Morris Petch and John O'Flaherty. She said she was never abused by Billy, and it's true that I never saw him abuse her and, as I said, even at the House of Hell he and Mum wouldn't join in if she was there.

During the months of questioning, things became quite difficult between Paul and me. He was still in a state of shock and anger, and I was very snappy and abrupt with him. It was as though I was trying to push him away. I still felt, deep inside me, that I was dirty and that nobody could love me, and it was as if I was deliberately giving him an excuse to walk away from me. It was all I felt I deserved.

It's to his enormous credit that he stuck by me through this time, when his own emotions were churning and our lives felt like they could never be the same again. He says he never for one moment thought about leaving me, that what we had, our happiness, was just as precious to him as it was to me. But in the back of my mind, I worried that he would take the boys and find a girlfriend who didn't have all this baggage in her life, someone normal. All I have ever wanted is to be normal. To most people it won't sound like much of an ambition, but when you come from such a terribly abnormal family as mine, it's a huge goal.

Paul was struggling to come to terms with the enormity of what had happened, and with the fact that I had concealed so much for so long. We'd been together a long time, and I was suddenly telling him that everything he'd known about me and my family was false; that I'd carried the most terrible secrets throughout our relationship. Most of all, he had to work hard to control his anger: he wanted to go out and smash Morris Petch and John O'Flaherty into the ground, an instinct he channelled into his work with the Society Against Paedophiles.

He also had to take on a lot of responsibility at home. I was going to the police station at least once a week, usually for several hours at a time. Paul had to look after the children more than usual and it became impossible for him to work, with so much going on in our lives.

That we survived this difficult time means, I think, that our love is very strong, and that we are meant to be together. Paul never once turned against me, and I certainly gave him cause to. I felt he should reject me, and it was as if I was goading him into going. We had rows and we came close to splitting up. But he never once threw in my face anything about the secrets I'd kept; he never for a second suggested I wasn't worthy of his love. If we argued, it was because I was being stroppy and difficult. I was tense, under pressure, and still very worried about implicating Mum.

Throughout this time, she was still visiting us, and I told her what was happening. We heard on the grapevine that Morris Petch and John O'Flaherty had been taken in for questioning by the police, and that others were also being questioned. Mum knew that I was seeing the police on a regular basis, but she never asked what was going on. I felt I needed to reassure her that I would keep her involvement a secret, and I took the opportunity one day when we were on our own in the kitchen at my place. Mum and I both smoke, and the kitchen is the only room where I allow it, in order to keep the smoke away from the children and Paul.

As we sat there, lit cigarettes in hand, I simply said to her, 'Don't worry, I'm not going to say anything about you, Mum.'

She just said, 'Right.'

As usual, she showed no reaction and she didn't ask me anything else.

She seemed neither pleased nor surprised, and she certainly didn't show any sign that she was relieved to know that I wasn't going to tell everything about her.

She kept up a good pretence of her innocence in it all, though. On one occasion Paul was talking to her about my abuse, and she was agreeing with him about how terrible it was, and she even said she couldn't believe it had all been happening to us without her knowing. She started crying, and said, 'I can't believe they touched my daughters.'

She told Paul that she never thought Granddad King would abuse me and Heather because at the time he was raping her. Paul said afterwards, when everything finally came out, that she deserved an Academy Award for that performance, as well as the one she put on when she first heard about Tam raping Heather. She could, he says, be a double Oscar winner. The fact that she has a low IQ was used as part of her defence in court, and it's true, she isn't bright. But her IQ is not so low that she didn't know how to hide things, and how to lie like a first-rate actress. It wasn't self-denial. She knew exactly what she was doing.

At the time, I was glad she was being so clever about it, and so convincing. The better she could act, the less chance there was of Paul or anyone else finding out the full truth.

But I do remember thinking, when she was crying, that she was overdoing it. I thought to myself, *Say you weren't there, protect yourself. But don't get carried away, or you'll forget the truth.*

My feelings were split: I wanted her to stay in the clear in public, but I didn't want her to let herself off the hook completely and to start to believe her own lies.

What made me change my mind about telling the police about her? Once again, it was Paul being on the ball, and reading me better than I can read myself. We were talking about my childhood, and he asked me, 'Why didn't you tell anyone?'

I replied, 'I had no one I could tell.'

'But why didn't you tell your mum?' To him, it was the most logical thing of all. If my stepfather was abusing me, and letting other men abuse me, why didn't I simply tell my mum? In Paul's world, a mother is there to protect her children, and he felt that even though I was very young and my abusers were telling me not to tell anyone, I could have confided in her and she would have stopped everything, putting Heather's and my safety ahead of her relationship with Billy.

But he knew my mum, and although he got on all right with her, he had always said motherhood didn't come to her naturally. When I have been ill in hospital, he has even had to convince her she should visit me. I think, at this stage, he suspected that she turned a blind eye to the abuse, preferring to look the other way and not ask questions. He felt she must have known what was going on, and therefore colluded with it by doing nothing.

I didn't like the fact that I was still partly lying to Paul. I trusted him completely, and it was not for lack of trust that I didn't tell him about Mum. I was worried about how he would feel about her, how he would treat her, if he heard the truth. It had taken me so long to create this false image of my mother and at least she made some effort towards seeming normal these days. I didn't want to lose that. I had seen how angry Paul was about the men who abused me: I felt sure he'd feel that same anger towards her.

Eventually, one night when we were lying in bed watching a film, he asked me, 'When you were really small, who took you to these houses to be abused? Someone must have been taking you? Tell me the truth, was your mother involved?'

I was shocked. 'How did you know?' I asked him.

'I couldn't work out how you went to the House of Hell if you were living in Abernethy – I guessed she must have been with Billy when he took you.'

Paul had pieced it together; he knew there were too many holes in my story. But he had no idea about the depths of her involvement.

I broke down and told him. He was deeply disturbed: it was not a case of her turning a blind eye and helping to cover up for the abusers, she was one of them. He had not expected that, and it stunned him. It renewed his mixture of anger and complete emotional upset. He could hardly believe it: it was too much to take in at first.

I didn't on that night tell him everything, not the full

scope of who did what, when and where. But I told him enough for him to realise she was more than a bystander.

His next reaction was to wonder why I was still in touch with her, why I still saw her. At this time she was living in Dalkeith with yet another boyfriend and she was visiting us regularly.

'She's not coming in this house again,' he said. I was alarmed: I'd not prepared myself for being cut off from her. She was a bad mother, but she was my mother, the only one I would ever have.

Paul told me that I needed to tell the police about her. I could see that he was right, that all the pieces in the jigsaw would not fit until she was included. He has a very black-and-white view of justice, and thinks it should be served no matter who is involved. But I know it was a tough time for him, he was very emotional about it. Although he found it easier to hate her than I did, his feelings were more complex than those he had for John O'Flaherty, Morris Petch and all the Kings, because she was a part of his life, too. After all, she's the grandmother of Jordan, his son.

For me it was the hardest decision of all, but it was one I knew I had to make.

It took me a couple of days to psyche myself up to facing it, but finally I made the most difficult phone call I've ever had to make. I rang Mum and told her I needed to see her, on her own. Paul babysat, and we went out for a meal at a pub near where we live. We both ordered steak and as soon as the waitress brought it over and left, I said:

'Mum, I've told Paul all about what you did with the others. Now I'm going to tell the police.'

'That's fine. It's best if it comes out, anyway. It would have come out eventually,' she said flatly.

She didn't sound upset or worried. She didn't say she was sorry. As usual, she was matter-of-fact about it all, as if we were discussing something trivial. Perhaps she had thought it through, and had prepared herself for it all coming out if John O'Flaherty and Morris Petch were confessing. Or maybe she didn't think about it at all. But she showed no surprise, and she carried on eating her meal.

After a while she said, 'What's going to happen?'

I told her it would be all right. 'Don't worry, you won't go to prison,' I reassured her.

Of course, I knew that it would not be all right, and that she would go to prison, but I didn't see any point in her worrying about it. Again, she showed no reaction, and finished her meal. She ate it all. It was me who found it hard to swallow. My appetite had gone and I left most of it untouched.

My emotions were raging. I was desperately worried, knowing what was ahead of her. But at the same time I felt exasperated, almost angry with her, for her cool indifference. She didn't seem to care, just as she had never cared when we were little. I wanted to shake her, force her to show some emotions, some natural feelings. I didn't want her to be afraid, but even fear would have proved that she was reacting normally.

I watched as she cleaned her plate and commented on

how much she had enjoyed it. How could she enjoy it when I was unable to swallow a mouthful? Once again, I had to face up to her coldness. It seemed so unfair that I was feeling guilty about what I was doing, when she showed so little guilt for everything she had done.

When I got home I told Paul what had happened, and we agreed that I now had to tell Angela. He was very supportive and reassuring. I rang Angela and made an appointment. When I told her that I needed to talk about Mum's involvement, she was not surprised. I think Angela had guessed much earlier that Mum must have been involved, and I feel sure that John O'Flaherty and Morris Petch must have talked about Mum's involvement in their interviews. Before I made this call, Angela never once questioned me about Mum but I think she probably realised I was holding some things back. I'm grateful she never pressed me on it. I needed the extra time before I felt ready to tell Paul and Angela about Mum.

Now, finally, I was prepared to tell the whole truth – or so I thought.

12

Making the appointment to see Angela about Mum was the easy bit: getting there was much harder for me. I was more upset than I had ever been throughout the whole investigation, and that's saying something. I was weeping a lot, often finding myself in tears for no apparent reason, even when I was busy with normal chores. I found it very hard to sleep: images of Mum being questioned by the police, Mum in court giving evidence, Mum in prison, Mum unhappy, kept going through my head. I had never been in a courtroom apart from giving evidence against the two women who had attacked us in our home, nor had I ever visited a prison, so the pictures in my head came from movies and TV programmes, and they were all horrific. Whatever she had done to me, it felt unnatural to be turning on her. My instinct was still to protect her.

The first time I went to St Leonard's Police Station to

talk to Angela about her, I simply couldn't get out of the car. I started to cry. Paul had driven me there, and he quickly realised that I was too distraught to go through with it at that time. He drove me home, and rang Angela to change the appointment. When I calmed down, Paul and I talked about it, and I knew that I still had to go through with it.

A few days later I went up to the police station again. Paul dropped me off, and I went in on my own. But as soon as I was inside I knew I couldn't do it. It was such an enormous step, there would be no going back from it. I had felt no qualms about John O'Flaherty and Morris Petch, but this was so, so different. This was like ripping up the whole fabric of my life. I was terrified, I didn't know what the consequences would be, emotionally – for Mum or for me. I still thought I would do it, but I knew that I wasn't ready yet.

I saw Angela and told her I wasn't ready. She was very understanding, and drove me home. The third attempt was the same: I went in to see her, but faced with the reality of sitting down and giving a statement, I could not go through with it. Angela was endlessly patient, and again she asked if I wanted her to take me home. I said no. I didn't want to admit to Paul that I had failed again, so to kill time I walked home. It took about forty-five minutes and all the time my mind was racing, going over and over the mess I felt I was making of my own life. I felt such a failure for not being able to do it, but I knew that once I said those words, made that official statement, I would be turning all our lives upside down, unleashing a whole new set of problems for us. I knew Paul would be disappointed in me for not going through with it, because he felt the only way forward was to get everything off my chest. So when I got back and Paul asked if I had done it, I lied and said yes. I was very quiet, but he assumed that was just because I was so upset by the interview.

That night, I told him I was tired and wanted to go to bed early. I hadn't formulated any plans, but I was very tired and longing for it all to go away. I said nothing to make Paul, who is so sensitive to my moods, suspicious, but I looked in on my sleeping sons and kissed them lightly, making sure I didn't wake them. On my own in the bedroom, I pulled out my bottle of insulin and looked at it, almost longingly: *This bottle contains oblivion, peace, a way out of everything.* My only thought was that I couldn't go on. I couldn't make the statement, and yet I knew that would mean letting Paul and Angela down. I felt I wasn't being a good mother to Jordan, Ryan and Young Paul, I wasn't being a good partner to Paul, and I certainly wasn't being a good daughter. I felt worthless, scared.

I didn't know how it would all work out. I didn't want to die, but I didn't want to be where I was. I was ripped apart by what I had to do to Mum, and although Paul had been wonderfully supportive, I don't think he understood how difficult this last piece of my past was for me. It was much more black and white for him.

I didn't want to tell Paul I hadn't made the statement, but at the same time I didn't want to do it. I simply didn't feel I had the strength to do it. I know she has never been a proper mother, but that doesn't stop me feeling like a daughter. I just couldn't grasp the reality of being the one who put her in jail. Carefully, I pumped the entire contents of the bottle of insulin into my arm. And slumped down on the bed for the sleep I was so longing for.

When Paul came to bed he found me semi-conscious. He knows how to check my blood sugars, and when he did the pinprick test he could see they were dangerously low. He rang for an ambulance, and I was rushed into hospital with an oxygen mask on my face and the paramedics shouting at me to keep me awake. I was very, very ill, and later one of the doctors explained to me and Paul that stress can actually kill, and that I had been very close to death even without the insulin overload. Paul had been worried that I wouldn't make it, that my body was so weak and debilitated that it would not be able to withstand the extra burden of the overdose.

In hospital my blood sugars were still dropping, and I was put on a drip and made to eat something. I was only kept in hospital overnight and most of the next day, but once again I had to see a psychiatrist. This time I could tell the truth about the police investigation and the pending court cases. The psychiatrist's assessment was that I was no longer a danger to myself, and let me go home.

Again, I was faced with telling Paul the truth: that I hadn't managed to tell the police about Mum. He was upset that I had been so afraid of facing him that I had tried to take my life again.

'Why didn't you just say?'

I still didn't want to go to see Angela, and for a while I continued to make excuses not to. Then one day I started to look at it differently. I looked through the eyes of my own children, and I knew that if I didn't do anything about it, they might one day ask me why not. I knew that they would see it in the same black-and-white way that Paul did: she did wrong, very serious wrong, and she deserved to be punished. It was with the children in mind that I finally managed to meet with Angela and tell her everything. She was very patient with me, she understood how hard it was for me. I cried a lot while I was talking to her – I think I got through quite a few boxes of tissues.

This was the point at which I finally completely offloaded everything that had for years been dammed up inside me: Angela heard about all the sex and violence, everything. I could speak openly and honestly, whereas in my previous statements I had to be careful not to say anything that would implicate Mum. Before I was always cautiously weighing up what I could say in my interviews, to keep Mum out of what happened. I hadn't realised how much this put me under stress, how limiting it had all been in my telling the truth to Angela. I felt so much better, so relieved not to have to hide anything. Even so, I was adamant that I didn't want Mum to go to jail, and Angela said it might be possible to just use her as a witness, if she co-operated.

Heather was called in to see Angela again, and as usual we didn't discuss what she was asked about. But I'm sure the subject was Mum and Billy, and I'm also sure that Heather told Angela that they didn't touch her. She has always said this, and stands by it to this day. Although they orchestrated her abuse at the hands of the Kings, John O'Flaherty and Morris Petch, I never witnessed her being abused by Mum and Billy, and she was never in the same room when I was being abused by them.

It was a few weeks before the police interviewed Mum, in December 2005. She rang me a couple of times during this period, although not as much as she usually did. She was not angry about me going to the police, and at this stage she said nothing to reproach me. She'd just say: 'How are you doing? How's everyone?'

Initially, it looked as though Mum would only be used as a witness, and not charged. One of the prosecution lawyers said that Mum was also a victim, because of her own childhood abuse, and that she could be helped if she was co-operative regarding evidence against the others. At first this was a relief, it was what I had told Angela I wanted. I had told the truth, but Mum was not going to be punished for her crimes. I didn't have to feel guilty about her suffering.

But when I thought about it and talked it through with Paul, I was worried that this wasn't right. I thought about the children, and how I would, perhaps, one day, have to answer their questions: how could I look them in the eye and admit that I helped shield her from the consequences of her actions? I wondered how I would ever be able to rest, knowing that she had gone unpunished and was still, in all likelihood, drawn to and mixing with paedophiles. I'm not denying that Mum had a bad childhood, and I'm sure she was abused by Granddad and Jamieson, but I also believe she was a prime mover in what happened to me and Heather, not just someone who was frightened into turning a blind eye. I worried about her suffering, but she had never worried about me or Heather. Also, the abuse she suffered as a child would be horrific enough on a normal scale, but the sadistic violence at the House of Hell, which she often initiated, was way off the scale, and not comparable to anything she had to endure when she was little. Regardless of my own feelings of guilt, I knew I had to do what was right.

In the end, I wrote a letter to the Procurator Fiscal, who is the Scottish equivalent of the Crown Prosecution lawyer handling a case, saying that if she wasn't being charged, I wouldn't give evidence against any of them. She had confessed to everything, so there should never have been any doubt about her being charged. In fact, she told me that when she confessed, the two police officers who were interviewing her actually called for some senior officers and a psychiatrist to sit through the interviews: I think what they were hearing was so shocking that they needed to make sure that she was not on drugs, or drunk, and that she was clear about what she was confessing to.

I felt very guilty about what I had done, deeply guilty. Part of me knew I had done the right thing, the other part of me wished I had kept up the pretence that she was innocent, or at least gone along with the plan not to charge her. I don't know why I felt so sorry for her after everything she had done to me, but I had many sleepless nights. Paul reassured me I had done the only thing possible, and that if I had not told the truth I would have had to live a huge lie for the rest of my life. I could see the sense in what he said, but it didn't make it any easier.

It slowly dawned on me that this was going to be a very significant court case, something the public and media had never seen before. I realised that it was going to bring a lot of unwanted attention. I had never expected this but it was too late now to turn back and hide. Initially, I thought it would be like the case against Tam, my father. Heather gave a statement, he pleaded guilty, it went to court, then it was all over and he went to jail; no witnesses were called and Heather and I didn't go to court. But this had turned into a much, much bigger affair, and I had to face the fact that it would not be dealt with quietly, without the whole world knowing. It was clearly going to be an historic case and none of us could escape it. I had to spend weeks and weeks going over statements both with the police and the Procurator Fiscal: at times it was like having a full-time job, which I had to juggle with looking after the boys and our home.

The whole family was in turmoil. It was very hard, with so much stress and emotion flying around, to keep life normal for the children, and I think everybody suffered. When I was crying, little Jordan would say, 'Stop crying, Mummy. Me make you better', just like I would comfort him when he fell over or bumped himself. It was so touching that it made me cry more. Ryan was constantly being told to go to his room to play with his computer games or watch a DVD, because we were talking about things we didn't want him to hear. He knew some of the things that had happened, and he knew my mum well. To him she was 'Granny', and she had always bought him and Young Paul Christmas and birthday presents, even before Jordan was born. It must have been very confusing for him. As for Young Paul, he was going through adolescence, coping with what is a difficult time for any youngster, but for him there was the extra burden of everything that was going on at home. I knew it was an enormous strain for everyone and I felt very guilty for the upheaval I had caused them.

The police investigation into Mum started just before Christmas, and it was very hard for me to turn my mind away from what was going on and concentrate on all the usual Christmas preparations. But it was important that I did, for the sake of the children. I remember dragging myself around the shops, hearing all those relentless Christmas songs and looking at the sparkly decorations, and feeling that none of it related to me. I wasn't part of the festive season. It was the first Christmas I had ever spent apart from Mum: after Paul and I got together, she always came to us for Christmas Day. I had to blank out thoughts about her, and try to make the most of Christmas for the kids' sakes.

Apart from all the official stuff, rumours about my case were starting to circulate in the area, and people were asking me about it. I couldn't face talking to them. (One of the main reasons I am writing this book is so that everything is out in the open in full and I won't have to constantly answer questions.) I worried about Paul, too: he had been so supportive, but how would he feel if the whole world knew about my shameful past? People would question him too. Nothing felt private any more.

The police and the Procurator Fiscal had explained to me that my name and Heather's name would not be used in court, so complete strangers would not know who the victims were. But all our friends, neighbours and anyone who vaguely knew us would be able to put two and two together if Mum's name was used, even if it was not revealed that the two sisters who were the victims were also her daughters.

On top of these worries, I was having to face up to the fact that Mum would go to prison. I was extremely worried about her as she didn't seem to understand how serious it all was. I thought this was partly my fault: I had convinced her she would be all right. I almost convinced myself. I knew, rationally, that her crimes were so severe the only punishment could be jail, but at the same time I thought the judge might be lenient with her. I certainly never imagined she would get a longer sentence than Tam.

The worry affected my health. I stopped eating and my weight dropped to seven stone. My collar bones stood out in deep ridges and my clothes hung off me. I was vomiting a lot, possibly caused by my liver problems. The stress continued to affect my diabetes, and I had to make many trips to hospital to stabilise my blood sugars.

It took eighteen months for the case to be prepared, and although the number of interviews I had to give to the police and the lawyers tailed off, Angela kept in touch about the progress of the police investigation. During all this time I still saw Mum, although not as much as before. At first Paul would not allow her into our home, so I used to go and meet her somewhere. It was always me who rang her: she never made contact with me. I was worried about her as she was drinking heavily. As time went on she became more anxious. She didn't show it much, but I knew this was the case because she started making sarcastic comments. She'd also say things like, 'You'll be glad when I'm in prison', and 'How would you feel if you were on your way to prison?'

I didn't answer her, I was prepared to sit back and take it if it made her feel better. Paul was with me once when I visited her, though, and when she had a go at me he spelled it out to her: 'You put yourself in this position, Caroline,' he said. 'Dana isn't putting you in prison. You did it yourself.'

Although, outwardly, she showed no sign of being very worried, it became clear that she was more deeply affected than everyone had realised when she tried to kill herself. I was in hospital with diabetic complications when Angela came to see me to break the news that Mum was also in the same hospital, the Edinburgh Royal Infirmary, having taken an overdose of paracetamol. Angela took me to visit Mum, who was in the high-dependency unit, barely conscious. She could hardly talk, but she would have had little chance to anyway: I was so upset that I went mad at her.

'What are you doing stuff like this for? Don't you think we've all got enough to cope with? Don't be so stupid. I love you, don't I? Why are you trying to make life even harder for me?'

I was not exactly rational, and my anger just exploded out of me: 'It's you that's put us all in this place. Now you want out of it. That's not fair.'

She tried to tell me that she had only taken a couple of paracetamol, but when I talked to the nurse I was told she had taken at least thirty-six. So it was a very real attempt to kill herself, not just a cry for help. She was in a pretty bad way, and I was told that it was highly probable, if she hadn't been found when she was, that she would have died.

I visited her every day, which was easy as I was still in hospital myself. After a couple of days in the high-dependency unit she was moved on to a ward. She was very yellow. An overdose of paracetamol causes severe damage to the kidneys and liver. Her liver is probably impaired for life. I believe she was drinking heavily at this time, which would have aggravated the damage.

After that first visit, when she was semi-conscious and I was angry with her, I told her never to do anything like this again – only this time I told her gently. Later, in court, her defence solicitor said she had made several suicide attempts, but I think I would know if there were any others, and this is the only one I heard about.

While I was sitting at her bedside I couldn't help but think about what lay ahead of her, and I have to admit that it passed through my mind that death could have been the best thing for her, but I quickly banished the thought.

It was during this long waiting game that Alan Kay came back into our lives. He had served his time in prison and I never wanted to see him again, but I bumped into him at a shopping centre. I would have walked on without talking to him, but he insisted on speaking to me.

'Dana, Dana, don't ignore me, hen. I need to speak to Paul urgently. It's a matter of life and death.'

I thought he was being melodramatic. When he said that the only place they could meet was on a garage forecourt, under the lights and the CCTV cameras, so that nobody would ever be able to accuse him of threatening or attacking Paul, I was convinced he was being paranoid, but I passed his phone number on to Paul.

Paul agreed to meet him. Alan told Paul that Paul's life was in danger. Paul was busy at this time running the Society Against Paedophiles, so we always knew that his safety was at risk, and I begged him many times to give up the campaigning. But he sincerely believes that the only way to counter the activities of paedophiles is to shine a bright light on them, to show them up to the world. It may not stop the way they feel, but it will make it harder for them to hide away and act out their sick fantasies.

According to Alan, a group of paedophiles, including my

mum, were plotting to get hold of a gun and shoot Paul. It had started with loose, boastful threats made by Alan (yes, she was back in a relationship with him, and was apparently also sharing sexual favours with Rab Heath again). Some of the paedophiles, all of whom had a vested interest in getting rid of Paul – who had been instrumental in several arrests, including Alan's – were taking Alan's ideas seriously, and now he was worried that it was getting out of hand. He said he didn't want to go back to prison, and certainly not for murder.

Alan told Paul that if he heard any rumours of his involvement in a plot against him, he should know that all Alan had done was make idle threats, and he had no intention of acting on them. On the other hand, he felt Paul was in real danger, as some of the others were serious. They planned to wait outside the back of the ice rink, where Paul always parked when he went to pick up Young Paul, who is a very good skater. It's a dark area, ideal if anyone really was trying to harm Paul. Only someone who knew his movements well – such as Mum or Alan – would have known that was where he parked.

Paul reported what he had heard to the police, who thankfully took it seriously. They fitted a panic button in our home, but nobody could be arrested because there was no real evidence, and Alan wasn't about to risk going on record with what he'd said to Paul.

It did nothing to ease my fears for Paul's safety. By this time the Society Against Paedophiles had ten cars on the road with blacked-out windows and, inevitably, they attracted trouble. Members didn't carry weapons, but they did have bulletproof and stab-proof vests, because they were vulnerable to attacks. On one occasion superglue was poured into the locks of one of the vehicles, and another had its windows smashed. More worryingly, one of the vehicles was attacked by men with baseball bats, and one member of the society had petrol poured into his home through an air vent.

I pleaded with Paul to stop, because I genuinely believed his life and the lives of all our family were in danger. I told him I could not take any more stress. While he was running the society, the paedophiles occupied him from dawn to dusk, there was nothing else we could talk about. He couldn't understand why it was so difficult for me to come out with every detail of what had happened to me, and he kept on about it, as though he were picking at a scab. He wasn't happy because he felt he was doing all this for me, and yet I was fighting it.

'This isn't helping my life right now,' I would say to him.

'But it's for you that I'm doing it,' he'd tell me.

I hated the fact that every waking moment in both of our lives was occupied by thoughts of child abuse. It was bad enough to be going through all the evidence Heather and I had to give, and to keep on giving, to the police and the Procurator Fiscal. It seemed even worse that Paul was on a crusade, not just about my case, but against every paedophile who ever walked the earth.

The phone was always ringing, he was going out to meetings, he was at risk of being attacked. I was constantly afraid for him, as well as being worried for myself. The stress on both of us was huge, and I begged him to give up his campaign. We rowed about it several times, and it was at this stage that our relationship was at its rockiest.

Looking back, it seems strange that we weathered the big storm – me admitting what had happened – but our commitment to each other nearly collapsed on this. I think we were both overwhelmed by the enormity of the disruption to our lives, and Paul just found a different way to cope. I believe running the society made him feel proactive, and gave him a sense of control, of being in charge. I understand his need: coming to terms with what had happened to his lover and partner must have made him feel emasculated, and he desperately wanted to put it all right again. He was, genuinely, doing it for me, and he couldn't understand why I wasn't grateful and supportive of the society.

I'm relieved to say that eventually, before the court case involving Mum started, he wound the society up. The police finally got through to him that the best way to tackle the paedophiles was through the courts, like I was doing. Paul realised it was important not to do anything that might compromise what was going to happen in court, especially if it became known that he was the partner of one of the victims.

His high-profile campaigning did have some very good results. He had letters from sex offenders thanking him for making the problem so public, and helping to give them the strength to do the right thing. He still feels very strongly about it. He says: 'If I put my children into the lion's den at the zoo, my children would be taken away from me because I had exposed them to danger. But I know where the lions are, where the danger is, so I don't expose my children to it. I don't know where the paedophiles are, I don't know when my children are exposed to danger. The authorities know where many of them are, but they're not telling. The paedophile has more rights than a small child has.'

Once the society was wound up, Paul and I started to get on better. But he still found it hard to understand why I kept in touch with Mum. It was clear-cut for him: she was evil, she had done evil things to her children, and we should all turn our backs on her. I tried to explain. 'I'm not asking you to like her, I'm not asking you to mix with her, I'm not asking you to let her see our children. But don't interfere with how I feel about her, because I can't help it. She's my mum, I love her.'

13

As if life were not terrible enough, there was another big blow in store for me.

Although we had moved apart and didn't see each other often, Catherine and I remained best friends until, tragically, she died. She was a drug user, and when she was twenty-five years old she was buzzing gas (inhaling butane gas from an aerosol can) when suddenly her organs simply shut down. She had got herself in with the wrong crowd, and her life had gone the wrong way.

Perhaps I had a premonition of her death, because, although we only saw each other every few months, a couple of days after her death I rang to see if she wanted to meet up for a night out. Paul was going to babysit as a treat so that I could get away from everything that was going on in my life. When I rang her home her mum answered and, not realising who I was, said, 'Catherine's not here any more.'

I thought she meant Catherine had moved out so I said, 'Where's she living?'

That was when I heard the terrible truth. She broke down and wept as she told me that her beloved daughter, and my best friend, was dead.

I went to the funeral home to see her in her coffin, and it was one of the saddest things I can ever imagine doing. She looked peaceful, and in some ways she was the Catherine I knew. But she had always been so full of life, so vibrant: it was awful to see her lying there, cold and still. I had seen death before: I had seen both Nana and Paul's mum in their coffins. But they were old, and although their deaths were sad, they were not unexpected. The death of one of my childhood friends was deeply shocking. She was my only real pal of my own age, she'd been part of my life for so long. I couldn't believe she had gone. It was such a waste of a young life.

When I got home from seeing her, I passed out. I think it was the shock, the stress of everything else that was going on, and my blood sugars were all over the place. Paul forced me to drink something sweet and gave me some insulin, so I didn't need to go to hospital.

That night I couldn't sleep. In fact, I didn't sleep properly until after the funeral. All I could think about was her mum and dad, their happy little family unit which I had envied so much when I was young. Now it was shattered. At the funeral they were in pieces, and there was nothing I could say that would comfort them; I felt so inadequate.

This was probably the lowest point in my entire life.

I felt like I was losing everything. My mum was going to jail, my best pal was dead, and my family's happiness had disappeared.

I wish I had seen and cherished Catherine more in those final few months. She was, and will always be, my best friend. It was from her family that I developed a very strong belief that there was a different and better life to the one that my parents inflicted on me and Heather.

I owe them a huge debt, and I will never forget that. I think about Catherine all the time: her face comes into my mind at odd times, when I am not expecting it, and I fill up with tears. I have lost a great deal in my life, most of it too soon for me to even know that it wasn't there. But Catherine's death was acutely painful, and always will be.

The case against Granddad came to court at the beginning of 2006.

Even though I had now told the truth about his abuse, the Procurator Fiscal decided that the charges of rape and assault on Heather were strong enough on their own, and they didn't charge him with any offences against me. Instead, fifteen charges of raping me were left 'on file', which means that if he ever re-offends they can be brought up against him.

Granddad pleaded guilty, admitting charges of rape and indecent behaviour going back more than ten years.

Paul and Angela went to court that day, but I didn't go and neither did Heather. Because he pleaded guilty, her statement was all that was needed, so at least he didn't put Heather through the stress of giving evidence in person.

Out on bail before he was sentenced, Granddad went to live with Mum in Micklefield where she had moved into another council flat. After Granddad was first arrested and bailed, she had been thrown out by her horrified boyfriend, who could not believe she was supporting him. She had immediately gone to live with Granddad. Later, she moved into a flat with her new boyfriend, where they were joined by Granddad.

After everything Granddad had admitted doing to his granddaughters, she still took him back into her home. She may have stopped abusing me physically after Billy died, but her morals had not changed, and she was perpetuating the abuse through her behaviour. She still had no feeling for what being a mother involves.

She and Granddad had to leave the flat where they were living after a crowd of local people, alerted to the fact that a child abuser was in their midst, attacked the property. Luckily the police arrived before anyone was physically harmed, and Mum and Granddad were taken into protective custody. They were each put into temporary bed-and-breakfast accommodation.

At this stage I was very worried about Mum because I had no idea where she was. She made no contact with me, and I didn't know how to contact her. Someone even told me that she had been seen working as a prostitute, and I made Paul drive me down to the area of Leith where the prostitutes usually work their trade, to look for her. There was no sign of her, and when I asked her about it later she said she hadn't been there. I wasn't convinced: I don't think there's much she wouldn't do. If we had found her that night I would have put her in the car and taken her home with us. I was terribly distressed at the idea of her selling herself on the street, putting herself at such physical risk.

After a few weeks living in emergency bed-and-breakfast accommodation, Mum was given another council flat, and she and her boyfriend moved back in together. I found out where she was and continued to see her every so often. Paul came to accept that it was impossible for me to cut her out of my life completely. She was still my mother, and I was torn apart by it all. I know the facts, I know what she did was wrong, and, if it was anyone else, I would be as unforgiving as I am towards my other abusers. But there's part of me that wants to take care of her, make everything right for her.

When Granddad, William Dunsmore, came up for sentencing two months after his trial, the judge said he had been guilty of an appalling breach of trust by taking advantage of Heather.

'This had very serious consequences for her. She has suffered considerably,' he said.

The judge told Granddad, who was sixty-nine at the time, that his behaviour made a prison sentence inevitable, and gave him five years. He was taken to Peterhead Prison, famous for its housing and treatment of sex offenders.

Of the 300 men in the prison, which is 165 miles north of Edinburgh, more than half are sex offenders.

I didn't feel bad about what happened to Granddad. It was fair, and he had it coming to him. In fact, in view of what has come out since about the way Heather was treated, he got off very lightly. As for Heather, she wasn't upset. Heather lives for the day. She understands that what Granddad did to her was very wrong, and she knows she did the right thing by speaking up about it. In that way she was more courageous than I was: she set the whole ball rolling. It was thanks to her persistence that I eventually faced up to the truth.

Mum didn't seem upset that Granddad went to prison, but perhaps she simply never showed it. She kept in touch with him, and even somehow scraped together £100 to give him at Christmas, far more than she has ever given to me or to Heather.

I am horrified that she is so forgiving and supportive of him. I know that I find it hard to distance myself from her, but if I thought she had touched my children, I wouldn't have any ambiguous feelings towards her: I would hate her and I would be unstoppable in my crusade against her.

But she seems able to forgive Granddad, not just for what he did to her as a child, which is hers to forgive, but for what he did to me and Heather. That's the bit I cannot take, because it's not hers to forgive. I've talked to her about it, and she cried when she told me about how he abused her when she was little.

I said: 'If you remember how unhappy you were when he

was doing it to you, how could you allow these atrocities to happen to your own daughters? It's not normal. If I suffer from headaches, I don't want my children to have headaches, too. If someone shoots a gun at me, it doesn't give me the right to shoot a gun at my neighbour. Just because you were abused, what made you want it to happen to your own children? You should have fought even harder to protect us.'

She cried more, but she could not explain it.

After Jordan was born I knew I wanted another baby, and so did Paul. But then our lives became immersed in the rounds of police interviews, visits to the Procurator Fiscal's office, and Paul's campaign against paedophiles. We weren't leading normal lives.

Because of all this pressure, Paul didn't think it was the right time to have another baby. I was worried that, because it had taken so long with Jordan, I might not find it easy to get pregnant and carry a baby to term again. I felt that the longer I left it, the harder it might be. So Paul agreed that we should try for another one, and to my amazement and delight I got pregnant more or less straightaway.

It was the best thing that could have happened. Somehow, my pregnancy seemed to settle the storm between us. We had something else to think about, apart from the past. It seemed like a real sign that we were going forward, that our lives were not completely dominated by dreadful memories and Paul's crusade. I became more relaxed about everything.

Unlike my pregnancy with Jordan, though, having Dylan was not straightforward, and I spent a great deal of the next few months in hospital. I think the combination of the stress I was under as the court case against Mum drew nearer, plus the difficulties with my diabetes, which went out of control during the pregnancy, made me far more ill than before.

When I was ten weeks pregnant I started bleeding heavily, and I was rushed into hospital. Because I was less than twelve weeks pregnant I was taken to the gynaecology ward, not the maternity department. I was very miserable, convinced that once again I was going to miscarry. Having Jordan had proved to me that I was capable of carrying a baby to full term, but I was still very panicky, as any mother would be. Paul was with me, and although it was a terrible time for us, we instantly got back our old closeness, both of us more worried about the unborn baby than about anything else that was going on in our lives.

I spent a few days lying flat and quiet in hospital and, thankfully, the bleeding stopped and I was allowed to go home. But that was just the first of several stays, usually because I was bleeding again. I was going regularly to the diabetic pregnancy unit, and whenever the staff there were worried about my blood-sugar levels I'd be admitted for a few days.

My diabetic nurse was – and still is – Janet Barclay, and here I want to pay tribute to her. Like Auntie Brenda and Angela, she is one of my heroines, one of the people who have helped me through the last few terrible years. She has always been acutely aware of the problems both Heather and I have managing our diabetes, and I have always been able to walk into the diabetic unit and see her, even without an appointment. But her support has gone far beyond just helping with the physical problems of diabetes.

I've never found it easy to talk to anyone about what happened to me, but with Janet I was able to open up about my feelings. Sometimes, it's easier to talk to someone who isn't involved. Paul was my greatest support, but at times he was too close. It was personal for him. And he had a different point of view, especially about Mum. Angela, too, was professionally involved. I'm not criticising her in any way: if you ask me who supported me most, after Paul it would be Angela. But Janet was different, she had no angle on it. She was just there for me. I could talk to her casually, without worrying about the case or her views on how I should react, and I could tell her anything. Chatting to Janet was therapeutic.

I didn't want to go into details about the abuse with Janet, but I could talk to her about my confused feelings. I could also – and this was the best bit – talk to her about normal things. She had a baby, not long after I had Dylan, and we met up while she was on maternity leave to have a coffee and to take our children to a children's farm. We chatted about nappies and sleepless nights and feeding problems – everyday things for new mothers, things that made me feel normal. She was (and still is) a really good friend, someone who extended a hand to me when I most needed one. Nobody will ever appreciate how good it was for me to have whole conversations without the abuse I had been subjected to and my mum being the main subjects. Later, Janet offered to look after my children when I had to go to court and, although I didn't need to ask her, I will always be grateful to her for the offer. Whenever I was admitted to hospital, Janet would come up to the ward a couple of times a day just to see me. Just knowing I had someone like her to rely on was a huge reassurance.

At this stage I had very little contact with Mum, and she didn't know I was having another baby until seven months in to my pregnancy. I think there was so much going on with the pregnancy that I didn't have time to dwell on the fact that I wasn't in touch with her, and, for Paul's sake, I was trying to keep a distance.

One day, I was at the hospital with Paul and Heather for one of my regular check-ups at the diabetic pregnancy unit. Paul went to collect the car and bring it round to the front entrance. He seemed to be taking a long time, so I called his phone and he told me he'd bumped into my mum. Heather and I went to meet them; we all went to the hospital cafeteria and she bought us a cup of tea. It was awkward, but friendly. I told her about the complications with my pregnancy, and she asked about the rest of the family. One good thing about Mum is that she never differentiated between Paul's kids and Jordan: she treated them all the same.

But it was a stilted conversation, and when we left there was no arrangement to meet up again.

Five weeks before Dylan was due I was in hospital, resting

and trying to get my diabetes back under control, when my waters broke. I was taken to the labour ward, but as contractions had not started, I was sent back to my own ward – not for long, however, as I started to bleed. I was taken back to the labour ward, where I began to have gentle contractions. The staff wanted me to hang on to my baby as long as possible, as he was obviously too early, but after four days of this gentle labour the contractions became stronger, and my baby was obviously in distress: his heartbeat was half the rate it should have been, and dropping.

Once again, I was rushed in for an emergency Caesarean. When Dylan was delivered, on Hallowe'en 2006, the cord was wrapped around his neck twice. He was whisked away before I could have even a glance at him, and the medical staff seemed to be working on him for ages. I was beside myself: I was convinced there was something seriously wrong with him. After what seemed like an eternity, he was brought back to me, all cleaned up and beautiful, weighing only four pounds three ounces.

Despite his difficult start, Dylan was perfect. This time we chose a name that we both liked – Dylan – and gave him John as a second name, after Paul's father. He had to spend a little time in an incubator, because he was jaundiced, but he fed normally and responded brilliantly. Janet, my diabetic nurse, came up to the ward and whisked him away to show him off to everyone in the diabetic unit. I'd spent so long in hospital that lots of the staff knew me, and they were all coming to visit for 'a wee look'. He was so small he looked drowned in normal baby clothes, but my lovely neighbour came to visit with some tiny baby-grows, specially made for premature babies.

Angela came to see us, too, bringing a present for Dylan. The one person who did not come was Mum, and she never gave me any presents for her new little grandson. It was such a hectic time that I didn't get too upset about her not being there, and didn't ring her to say she had another grandchild. But there were moments when I missed her, especially when I saw other young women who had had babies at around the same time as I had, with their mothers by their bedside, cooing over the new arrival.

After two days I begged the staff to let me take him home. I had spent so much time in hospital that I just wanted to get back to my family, whom I'd missed greatly, and to normal life. I had to wait for Dylan to have a blood test to show that the jaundice had gone, but then we were able to go. It was evening by the time Paul drove us home, but I didn't care. I simply wanted to be back in my own home.

The other children have been great with Dylan. When Jordan was born, I made a point of involving Ryan, and I did the same this time with Jordan. As far as he is concerned, Dylan is his baby. He helps bath him, fetches clean nappies, plays with him. Naturally, there have been one or two occasions when Jordan has wanted to sit on my knee when I have been feeding or cuddling Dylan, but I've always managed to make space for him.

Finally, I felt complete: I had my own two lovely little boys, as well as Paul's two. We were a happy family unit, and I knew that nothing would break us. I had a new baby to concentrate on, and that put all my other worries and fears into perspective. Having Dylan was such a great thing for me and Paul: it brought us back together and helped us to recognise the real priorities in our lives again. He is so special: a baby who brought his mum and dad back to the closeness we had always had before this huge storm erupted in our lives. He has healed a lot of pain and pulled us through a really bad time.

14

Against the background of my new-found contentment, the criminal investigation surged on. In February 2007, four months before the main trial, Mum, John O'Flaherty and Morris Petch came up at Edinburgh High Court to be charged. I didn't want to go, but Paul did. The whole case was outlined in a public hearing, so that the following day a very detailed story appeared in the *Edinburgh Evening News*. It revealed that up to fifteen adults had been involved in this paedophile ring, and that other cases would follow. It went into the general evidence against the others, who were not named, including the blindfolded rape at Abernethy, and the gang rape of Heather by five men on the day before her sixteenth birthday.

The three accused were named and the charges against them were listed. Mum faced twelve sets of charges, including raping me, molesting me, beating me with a belt and having sex with various men in front of me. (A woman can legally be charged with rape if she allows a man to rape someone and does nothing to stop it.) Morris Petch was charged with six sets of offences, including raping both me and Heather and forcing us to commit indecent acts with each other while he watched. John O'Flaherty faced four sets of charges, including multiple rapes of both of us.

In the outline of the evidence the court was told about Billy, Granddad and Nana King abusing me with Mum. So even though they were dead, at least some justice was coming their way: their crimes were being exposed to the world.

At that time, all three of them pleaded not guilty. It was revealed that the victims were two sisters, but it was not revealed that Caroline Dunsmore was our mother nor that Billy was our stepfather.

But, of course, everyone who knew our family instantly knew who we were. I felt embarrassed at first: my worst fear, for many years, had been that people would know what had happened to me. I had dreaded it all coming out into the open. It had been very difficult for me dealing with Paul knowing, and now I had to face so many other people. Seeing it in black and white, covering almost a whole page of the local newspaper, was horrible: it suddenly seemed very real. I knew then that there would be no hiding place for me: all my secrets were about to explode into the open.

I was worried about how people would react to me. I still couldn't shake the feeling of being dirty just through association with these dirty people. But the reaction was very heartening. Everyone was very nice, a lot of people said supportive things. I remember a woman I knew by sight coming up to me in Asda asking, 'Was it you in the paper?'

When I said yes, she patted my arm and told me how well I had done. Over the course of the next few months, as more and more people discovered who I was, I received lots of letters, mainly from people who had had similar experiences to me. Initially, too, I'd had some letters and cards from friends giving me and Heather their support. It means a lot to me that people have gone to the trouble of sending their kind thoughts and reassurances.

But inevitably, I suppose, there were a couple of nasty incidents. Paul and I were dropping a friend off in the Calder area of Edinburgh when Denver Petch, the man whose presence on my doorstep that fateful night had triggered the darkest of my moments, spotted me and came across to our car, shouting: 'Don't you mention my brother – he's not involved!'

His son was with him, and was also shouting abuse at me. Paul wound the window down and yelled back, but I just said to Paul, 'Let's go. Ignore them.' We drove off.

On another occasion Billy's niece, who's about the same age as me, started verbally attacking me when I was out shopping.

'I can't believe what you're saying about my family. And nobody else will believe you, you liar,' she said. She wasn't yelling it out loudly, but her tone was very aggressive and I felt threatened.

I just carried on walking, and when I got home I told Paul. He was angry, and he rang Alan King, her father, and said, 'Tell your daughter to back off and stop giving Dana a hard time.'

It was around this time that Paul bumped into John O'Flaherty at the market. Paul went there to see one of his brothers and John O'Flaherty was also working that day. Paul knew John O'Flaherty: he had lived near to him years earlier. I had always worried that if Paul bumped into one of my abusers he would not be able to contain his anger. But he was very cool. He went up to him and said, 'Do you know who I am?'

John O'Flaherty said he did and, remarkably, he didn't try to get away from Paul. Then Paul phoned me, told me who he was with, and handed the phone to John O'Flaherty. I spoke to him. It was a shock, hearing him say hello, and part of me wanted to hurl the phone to the ground. But I said, 'I just want to ask you one question. Did you think I would never grow up?'

There was a silence at the other end, then he muttered that he was sorry. I didn't want to talk to him, and cut the call off. He repeated to Paul that he was sorry, and Paul said, 'I expect you'll be going to the police now.' John O'Flaherty said he would, and that he would give a full confession, which he did. It doesn't redeem him in my eyes, I think he was only trying to do the best for himself with his confession, and by helping the police with their investigations into the others who were involved. It was self-serving, but nonetheless it has helped get other paedophiles into the dock.

So by the time of the court case, he had changed his plea from not guilty to guilty, and so had Mum. Both of them were prepared to give evidence against others, although John O'Flaherty couldn't give evidence against Morris Petch because they weren't involved in my abuse together. However, both he and Mum have helped by giving evidence against the people who are still being investigated. John seems to derive from this a feeling that he is better than the others, but as far as I am concerned his offers of help are given only to help himself. I'm glad he is co-operating with the police, but I don't believe it diminishes his own involvement.

If Morris Petch had also pleaded guilty, there would have been no need for a huge trial, and Heather and I need not have been involved, apart from giving our statements. That's how it had happened with Tam's and Granddad's cases. But Morris Petch was in denial – and still is, to the best of my knowledge. By his decision to plead not guilty he was inflicting cruelty on me and Heather right to the end. Not content with abusing us as children, he abused us again through the legal process. It was his right, of course, and although I hated him for it, I was determined it was not going to give him another victory over me. I knew I was strong enough to do whatever was needed to get him behind bars for a very long time.

I'd never been to the High Court until a couple of weeks before the case, when a woman from the Edinburgh Victim Support agency took me and Heather, together with Heather's social worker, on a conducted tour. The court building is old, but it has recently been modernised and given a glass roof, so that inside there is a light, airy feel to it. There is a marble-lined foyer, and a wide imposing staircase up to the courts. Court One, where the case was heard, has big wooden doors. The victim-support woman showed us where the judge and jury would sit, and the dock where the defendants would be. For me, the important bit was where the witness box was, because that was where I would be standing to give evidence. Heather was allowed to give evidence by a CCTV link from another room, because of her vulnerable status.

Seeing an empty courtroom wasn't frightening or awe-inspiring: to me it was simply an empty room. It didn't seem real.

On the Saturday before the trial started I panicked about what I was going to wear. I'd thought I would go in my normal clothes, but I realised that, being a full-time mum, almost everything I have is casual. I wear jeans and tops most of the time, and so does Heather. I wanted us to look smart, to show how important the event was, so we went shopping for 'court clothes', and I bought a black trouser suit, and Heather bought a navy pin-striped trouser suit. We both wore plain white shirts: we probably looked like a couple of lawyers.

My anxiety levels before the trial were enormously high. I could not hold any food down – if I ate, I vomited. Paul took me to see the doctor three times in one day, but they could find nothing physically wrong with me.

As the day got nearer, the pressure inside me built up.

I didn't show my feelings. Although Paul could see I was physically unwell, every time he asked me I told him I felt OK. He was pleased that everything was finally coming to court. I, on the other hand, was dreading it, but I found it hard to admit to my fears.

I wasn't sure how much Heather understood, but I talked to her about Mum. I told her Mum would go to prison. She asked 'Will she be all right?' All I could say was 'Yes, she'll be all right. She'll be looked after.' I was worried sick myself about what would happen to her, but there was no point telling Heather my fears. She can't understand what going to prison will really mean for Mum and, to be honest, she's better off not knowing.

The day before the trial, Paul was out and I was feeling desperate. I felt I couldn't go through with it, and thoughts of suicide began preying on my mind again. Worried, I took Heather, Jordan and Dylan round to Gail and Tony's house. Tony came outside to meet us, and he could see before I even said anything that I was in a bad way. The same thought kept running through my head, on a never-ending loop: 'If I hadn't told on her, this wouldn't be happening.' No matter how many times I told myself that she deserved it, I couldn't banish this thought.

'Can you look after the kids while I go to the doctor's?' I asked him. Of course he and Gail were happy to have them, but I still needed to make an appointment to see the doctor. I rang on my mobile, but frustratingly, having finally acknowledged I needed help, I was told there were no appointments available. I was getting very distressed, so

Tony took the children into the house. I told the doctor's receptionist that I was suicidal and that my need for help was urgent and couldn't wait. They sorted it so that a doctor could see me, and Tony drove me round to the surgery, two minutes away.

I was taken in to a young woman doctor I had never seen before. I was crying my eyes out by this stage, as if all the tension had suddenly been released and I could no longer control what I was feeling. Tony had to explain to the doctor what I was going through, and what I faced the next day, because I was sobbing too much to be able to talk. The GP prescribed Diazepam, a tranquilliser. She also gave me the phone numbers of counsellors, the Samaritans, and others she thought would be able to help me.

Just letting go of my pent-up feelings probably helped a lot, and I didn't actually take the tablets until the following day, when I had to go to the court. I cried for a few minutes in the car when we drew up at Tony's house, then pulled myself together so that the children wouldn't know how upset I was.

We were due at court at nine forty-five in the morning, and I'd been told I was going to be the first witness, so I would be giving evidence that day. I was very nervous. I got up really early, which wasn't difficult because I had hardly slept. I washed my hair, and then made sure everything was organised for the children. Young Paul, who was a very mature eighteen-year-old by this time, was going to look after them. I couldn't face any breakfast, so all I had was a cup of coffee.

Tony and Gail were coming with us, so they met us early at our flat. Heather's social worker arrived to take her, and the rest of us set off together. Tony and Paul both wore suits, I wore my new black suit. We looked as if we were going to a funeral, and in a way it felt like we were.

By the time we had found somewhere to park, we were just on time, and I was relieved: I was anxious not to be late, but I also didn't want to have to hang around too long.

As we went through the security check at the entrance to the building, I looked up and saw Morris Petch, leaning on the glass-panelled balustrade at the top of the stairs leading to the courtrooms. He must have seen me, but he didn't move away. I decided I wasn't going to hide from him or any of the others, so I walked up the stairs without looking at him, with my head held high, and passed within three feet of him. I was flanked by Tony and Paul, so I felt completely safe. He was very changed from the man who had abused me all those years before, and it took me a couple of seconds to recognise him. He had been skinny then; now he was big and fat, and had gone bald, and he was holding a walking stick. He was wearing a black shirt and black trousers, but he still looked scruffy. It was the first time I had seen him since my childhood, when he'd been abusing me.

As we turned left to go to the witness room, I was aware of Mum sitting on one of the blue benches round the walls of the foyer. I didn't turn and look directly at her, and she didn't look at me. But in the glimpse I caught of her I could see that she, too, had made an effort to dress smartly: her frizzy hair was well combed and she was wearing a dark trouser suit. It was almost as if she, Heather and I had all been shopping together: we were all wearing similar clothes. The sight of her brought a lump to my throat, and I quickened my pace to get inside the witness room, because I couldn't face looking at her or speaking to her.

We sat in the witness room with Angela and her colleague Callum Lamond, the detective sergeant who headed the investigation team (there were four police on the team, and they were known as the Amethyst Squad). I knew DS Lamond: he had been round to our flat when Paul was running the Society Against Paedophiles, and it was he who eventually persuaded Paul to disband it. I had also had to give a statement to him once when Angela was off work. He was very pleasant and professional, but I found it much harder talking in detail about the abuse to him than I did to Angela.

Heather and her social worker were already there when we arrived. Before the case started two of the lawyers came into the witness room to introduce themselves: one of Morris Petch's defence lawyers and Iain McSporran, the advocate depute (prosecuting counsel in English law) who would be leading the case against Mum and the others. I don't think it's usual for witnesses to meet the lawyers first, but because ours was such a sensitive case, and because Heather was classified as a vulnerable witness, an exception was made.

As he was leaving, the defence lawyer said, 'Don't worry, I'm used to dealing with frightened young girls.'

I replied, 'So's your client.'

He left without saying anything more. I felt his remark was condescending. I'm quite shy; until this case I'd never had to speak up for myself in public. I know I have a quiet voice, but I'm *not* a frightened little girl. I was, once, many years ago, when I was too small to defend myself. But not any more. Standing up to him helped steady my nerve and reinforced my determination to be strong.

We weren't allowed into the courtroom, as it was partly a closed case – the public and the press were excluded, apart from during the evidence of the police officers, the final submissions by the lawyers, the judge's summing up and the verdict. It was closed to protect the victims – me and Heather.

So all we could do was sit in the witness room. There was tea and coffee available if we wanted it, but my stomach was so tight I couldn't drink anything hot. Heather and I both carry a supply of sweet drinks like Lucozade in case we have diabetic hypos, and I sipped mine regularly. Every so often one of the victim-support people would come in and tell us what stage the case was at, and explain the procedure.

Most of the time we sat in silence. There was nothing much to say to each other, although Paul and Tony would both ask me how I was feeling from time to time. Heather chatted to her social worker, but even she was more subdued than normal.

Eventually, a court official came and told us that neither Heather nor I would be called to give evidence that day.

Instead of me being the first in the witness box as had been planned, Mum had given evidence first. She told the court that Morris Petch was a friend of Billy's, and that she and Morris Petch had sex together in front of a ten-year-old girl (me) and that Morris Petch then had sex with me. She said: 'Petch is guilty. He is just as guilty as me.'

Although we weren't needed, only Heather and her social worker left straightaway. The rest of us wanted to follow what was happening as much as we could from outside the courtroom. This meant we saw Morris Petch a couple of times: whenever there was a court break he was always hanging around the foyer and landings, or leaning on the glass security cubicle near the door. Because he was not being held in custody he was free to come and go during the breaks, and I had to walk past him.

I think this is wrong. I know he was technically innocent until proven guilty, but I feel that it is very unfair on witnesses, particularly in sensitive cases like this one, to have to mingle with the people they are giving evidence against.

At one of the breaks, I went round the side of the court building with Gail to have a cigarette. I know I shouldn't smoke, but this was such a stressful time I needed it to calm me down. Suddenly, I was accosted by several members of the King family. Apparently, they had tried to come into the court, but had been turned away. Now they began shouting at me, ranting and raving.

'Don't you go mentioning my family's name', 'Keep our family out of this', and that sort of thing. They swore at me a bit, and they were all getting steamed up. I was afraid they would attack us. Thankfully, when Paul and Tony saw what was happening, they ran over.

Paul told them, 'At the end of the day, your family played a big part in this. The best thing is for you all to go home.'

Before it could get any nastier, the court security staff, who had refused to allow them in the court building, came across and told them to move on or the police would be called. They went, still shouting the odd bit of abuse at me as we went back inside. They were not there next time we went out, and we didn't see them again during the trial.

During one of the breaks on that first day, John O'Flaherty was outside the courtroom. He looked relaxed and smiled at me, looking as though he wanted to come over and chat with me. I think he really believed that because he had given a full confession and was prepared to give evidence against my other abusers, I would be pleased to see him. I turned my back, and Tony said, 'Leave Dana alone, she's having a break. We don't want to see you hanging around.'

Just the sight of him caused me to shudder: for an instant I was back on the doorstep of that disgusting, dirty flat, a small child waiting in terror for him to open the door, trembling at the prospect of what was to come. I grabbed Tony's arm and he shepherded me away.

We didn't see Mum as we left: I didn't see her again until the third and final day, when all three of them were in the dock. The rest of the time, only Morris Petch had to be there as the other two were pleading guilty, so no evidence was presented against them, and they only had to return at the end of the case for sentencing.

The delay before my evidence was heard made it worse for me: I had to get through another very anxious, sleepless night. Even though I thought I would not be questioned about Mum, only about Morris Petch, I was still very nervous about giving evidence. I'm ashamed to say I was so preoccupied with my own fears that I didn't really take much notice of how Heather was coping. She has a really good social worker who was with her the whole time, and that's what Heather needs, a lot of attention. I think she coped better than I did with the delay.

On Wednesday, the second day of the trial, Heather again travelled with her social worker, and I went with Paul, Tony and Gail. This time I saw Morris Petch as we entered the building, and I noticed he was leaning heavily on his walking stick. I have since found out that he had had his leg amputated below the knee about five years earlier, after being thrown from a balcony. I made a point of looking straight at him, and he dropped his head and turned away from me.

Outwardly, I was strong and defiant, with my head held high. But, again, I had to suppress a painful flashback to the dark room of his flat, the walls covered in his grotesque paintings, and that filthy bed settee, permanently open and ready for Heather and me to be abused on. I could see the blank bewilderment on her little face as she and I were made to go through sordid routines for him. I pushed the thoughts out of my head: but at the same time, they reminded me what this case was really about. It was about terrible acts that had happened to two very young, innocent little girls, not words on a prosecution charge sheet.

I was called to give evidence soon after the court resumed. Paul squeezed my hand, Tony and Gail patted my back and wished me luck. I knew they were all supporting me, but I was shaking and felt very alone as I walked in through the big wooden doors of Court One, following the patient court usher. My legs felt weak, as though I was on the verge of collapsing, and every little bit of me was trembling. I was not frightened by the court or its formal procedures, just by the whole prospect of speaking up in front of people about something that to me was still steeped in shame. At the same time, I was determined not to let anyone see that I was afraid, so I breathed deeply and kept calm. Because it was a closed court, there were no family or friends in the public gallery to silently offer me their support. I was, as so often in my life, entirely on my own. But this time, I was determined to stand up to my abusers.

I was on the stand for an hour and twenty-five minutes, and it took me at least half an hour to relax. The prosecuting lawyer, Mr McSporran, questioned me about my childhood, and I found I had to talk about Mum and Billy, because it was impossible to talk about Morris Petch and not explain their role. I was relieved that Mum was not in court to hear me.

Morris Petch's defence lawyer cross-examined me, but the crux of his attack on my evidence seemed to be that I had something against Billy and I was taking it out on Morris Petch to get back at Billy. I couldn't see the sense in that argument. He said to me, 'I put it to you that you are lying.'

Eventually, after some more notions from him about why

I should be deliberately trying to incriminate Morris Petch, I said it back to him, 'I put it to you that *you* are lying.'

He was constantly trying to trip me up, but I could answer all his questions. It wasn't difficult because all I had to do was tell the truth. At one point, going through the harrowing bits, there were tears in my eyes, and I had to try very hard not to cry. I didn't want to give him the satisfaction of reducing me to tears. When I glanced at the jury, which was made up of seven men and six women, I could see that at least a couple of them had tears in their eyes, too. The judge never interfered with the questioning: he didn't have to, as I was able to answer everything.

When my evidence was over and I walked back to the witness room, I realised I felt clammy and sticky. I must have been perspiring, although I was not aware of it while I was in the court.

Everyone was waiting for me, and I had time to give Heather a cuddle and tell her not to worry, that it would all be OK. I kept calm until she was led away to give her evidence, because she takes her cue from me and I didn't want her to see me upset. But as soon as she had gone I collapsed in tears. I had stayed strong and focussed in the courtroom, but now I was shaking and crying uncontrollably. It took about half an hour for the others to comfort me back to calmness.

I was worried about Heather: if the defence lawyer was as fierce with her as with me, trying to trip her up and calling her a liar, Heather would either break down or she would get agitated and defiantly angry. She seemed to be in there for an eternity, but in fact it was only just over an hour, less time than my evidence had taken.

When she came back she was crying her eyes out, really upset, sobbing and clinging to her social worker and to me. I cuddled her, and then Paul cuddled her, and we all tried to calm her down. She needed lots of reassurance. She said she had been called a liar, and in Heather's childish eyes that's a terrible accusation, particularly when it is unjust. She could not possibly understand that it was the lawyer's job to try to trip her up and make her contradict herself. Again, I think the court system is wrong when it puts vulnerable people like Heather up for cross-examination. Even though she did it via CCTV, it was a truly terrible procedure for her to go through. And getting someone like Heather confused isn't difficult – it would be a much better system if she could simply tell her story to someone impartial. To her credit, I believe she did stick to the truth, but I know the whole process was very distressing.

As soon as she had calmed down enough, her social worker took her home. Heather bounces back easily from most of her upsets, and I knew that once she got away from the court atmosphere she would start to feel better. She didn't have to come to court again, and for that I was grateful.

For both of us, the worst was over. But for me there was still a lot of anxiety: I felt sure that Morris Petch would be convicted, but I couldn't relax until it was all over.

15

After what had been a long, harrowing morning, Paul, Tony, Gail and I went to get some lunch before the afternoon session began. Afterwards, I was standing outside the court, enjoying the fresh air and calming myself down with a cigarette when I found myself surrounded by journalists.

I was astonished at the media interest. I had never expected it to be so huge. I knew from the reaction when the charges were printed three months earlier that there were going to be headlines, but I didn't take on board the scale of it. But of course, by pleading not guilty Morris Petch had guaranteed maximum press coverage. The fact that a woman was involved (although at this stage it was not known that she was the mother of the victims) and the fact that the police had said that eventually there might be as many as fifteen people charged made it a much juicier case for the media than the normal run of court cases, even those involving paedophilia. There was already media speculation that this was the biggest paedophile ring ever to be exposed in Great Britain.

At first I was slightly frightened by the media scrum and I didn't reply to any of their questions. Tony stood in front of me until I finished my cigarette, then we went back in to court to hear Angela and her colleague DS Lamond give their evidence, which they gave in open court so that we could sit in the public gallery and watch and listen. There were a few other people there, and I looked round to see if there were any of Morris Petch's family, but I didn't recognise anybody.

Afterwards, the defence started, and Morris Petch's niece gave evidence on his behalf. The court was closed again for this, so I have no idea what she said, except that she was speaking in support of him. I knew her from when we were children, when I used to see her at Morris Petch's flat. Morris Petch himself didn't give evidence on his own behalf, probably because he didn't want to be cross-examined.

After the evidence was over, the prosecuting lawyer Mr McSporran came to talk to us. He said that he would bet his house on us getting a guilty verdict. In Scottish law, unlike in the rest of Britain, there are three possible verdicts: guilty, not guilty, and not proven. He said he didn't think there was the slightest chance of even a not-proven verdict.

Thursday, the third day of the trial, saw the lawyers making their final speeches and then the judge, Lord Malcolm, summing up. This all happened in open court, so this was when the press and public heard most of the details of the case against Morris Petch. We were in the public gallery, and I started to cry. It really hit home how terrible my childhood had been when I heard it all spelled out in the cold language of a courtroom. Phrases like 'horrific crimes' made me realise just how awful the abuse was, and how shocking it must sound to other, normal people.

It seemed to take the judge ages to tell the jury all the rules and regulations – it probably took him longer than it did for them to reach their verdict. They were only out for sixteen minutes, and they came back with a unanimous verdict of guilty to the charges relating to me, and a majority verdict of guilty to the charges relating to Heather.

When the word 'Guilty' was spoken by the foreman of the jury, Morris Petch turned to look up at the public gallery, and searched the faces until he found mine. The public gallery is above the dock, so he had to swivel right round and tilt his head back. His eyes locked on me and he gave me an evil glare. It really churned my stomach. He's a big frightening-looking man, but I was more sickened than scared. Gail and Angela were on either side of me, and they squeezed my hands. Tony, outraged by him daring to stare at me, muttered, 'Fucking animal.'

Tony told me afterwards that it really spooked him, seeing this evil man glaring at me. He also said that, although he had heard from Paul and me lots of the details of what happened to me, hearing it all spelled out so graphically made him realise just how appalling my childhood had been. He sat through the summing up with a lump in his throat, barely able to control his tears.

Lord Malcolm then said that all three of them – Morris Petch, John O'Flaherty and Mum – would be sentenced the next day, Friday 25 May 2007. Despite the guilty verdict on Morris Petch he was again allowed to go free on bail. After that glare, I dreaded seeing him outside the courtroom. Paul and Tony stuck close to my side as we left, but luckily Morris Petch was not around.

Mr McSporran came up to me as we left the court, and took me into a side room. He told me how proud he was of me for giving evidence so well, and that without me they would not have got a guilty verdict. He said I was one of the best witnesses he had ever had. I felt a warm glow of pride: it had been very difficult, but I had done it.

The next day, we went to court for the sentencing, but I couldn't face going in. I didn't want to see Mum being sentenced. I kept thinking horrible thoughts about what would happen to her. I was really upset, and I sat on a bench outside the courtroom with Gail.

The biggest drama was that Morris Petch failed to show up, and the judge had to issue a warrant for his arrest. The case carried on without him, with just John O'Flaherty and Mum in the dock.

She and John O'Flaherty had no previous convictions, but it turned out that Morris Petch had been given a thirty-month sentence in 1986 for assault with intent to rape. Mr McSporran summarised the case against Mum and John O'Flaherty, describing what happened to me and Heather as 'extraordinary' and 'quite incredible'. This part of the case was in open court, and was widely reported across all the national newspapers and Scottish television channels, so even though I wasn't in court, I have read what was said.

Mr McSporran said that when Mum was first interviewed by the police she claimed to have only gone along with what was happening out of fear of Billy, but then she volunteered a statement to the police in which 'she broadly accepted that she had participated freely in the abuse'.

John O'Flaherty admitted having sex with me twelve times, and that he knew other men were having sex with me. He also admitted being one of those who raped me in the mobile home at Abernethy, when I was blindfolded and screaming.

Mr McSporran said: 'It was pointed out to him that she [me] was nine at the time, but neither that nor his account of her screaming caused him to exhibit remorse, and the police describe him as "indifferent". It appears that not only had these girls become so accustomed to being raped that it was seen [by them] as a way of life, but their rapists saw it that way too, being utterly indifferent to the effects upon the victims, and not even particularly conscious of the gravity of their crimes. The damage caused by this history of abuse is impossible to quantify.'

He said he believed Heather had been more profoundly affected by it than I had, and that she needed ongoing counselling and support. He added that we had both considered suicide – when I read this I wanted to shout out that we had both actually attempted it.

In the end, the judge deferred sentence on Mum and

John O'Flaherty for four weeks, to allow background reports to be prepared on them. So I could have sat in without having to witness Mum's sentencing. In a controversial decision they were both granted bail. With Morris Petch on the run, the judge was later criticised by the media for risking their disappearance, too. But the defence solicitors argued that they had both turned up whenever required to, and that background reports were easier to prepare if they were free.

I saw Mum as she came out of the court, but she didn't look at me. She had to go a different way, to sort out her bail. I felt very upset for her, but at the same time I was angry that they were being released back on to the streets after they had been found guilty of such terrible crimes. It was a temporary relief because Mum still had a bit more freedom, but I don't believe guilty people should be given bail so easily, particularly when they are guilty of crimes against vulnerable children. It just seems too great a risk to be taking with our children's well-being.

I felt such a mixture of emotions. I was ecstatic that Morris Petch and John O'Flaherty were going to go to jail for what they had done to me, and if it had not been for Mum's involvement I would have been out on the streets dancing with joy. But because of her, I felt very sad.

I didn't see Mum again in the court precincts, but Paul did. She was talking to John O'Flaherty, and according to Paul they were both calm, chatting away as though they were friends who had just met up. Nobody would have believed they were facing charges of raping children.

You would have thought they were there for something as trivial as a driving offence. That's typical of Mum: still she didn't seem to take on board the seriousness of the situation she was in.

As we collected our things together to leave, one of the victim-support people came across and told me that there was a huge crowd of press outside. I didn't want to face them, so Gail and I were taken out by a side door. Tony and Paul went out the front way, where the police involved in the case were talking to the reporters.

Callum Lamond said, 'All three have never shown any signs of remorse to this day. When interviewed they disclosed the details so matter-of-factly. John O'Flaherty, in particular, spoke about it as if it was completely normal.

'I don't think they ever expected to be charged. It was the last thing they thought would happen after all this time. But Morris Petch was in denial. He wanted to blame everyone else, and that's why he pleaded not guilty. He couldn't admit it.

'The abuse took place in private houses. There were no drugs or alcohol involved. This was purely for their own sexual gratification. We've asked how it all came about, how it started; how the subject could be raised between them. But they've not been able to answer that. They say it just happened.'

He said the group seemed to shun social contact, and that Morris Petch was 'highly antisocial'.

Then he spoke about me and Heather.

'It's fair to say that, considering what they've been

through, the women have dealt with it well. They now lead fairly normal lives. They were looking forward to having this all come out in court.

'It was a huge step for them to break their silence to us. They hadn't even spoken to each other about it. The girls never made disclosures to social workers and they were never involved with the social work department. In the main, the people involved were not known to the police.

'It seems no one had reason to suspect there was something wrong. The girls thought what was happening to them was normal. They thought it happened to all children. They had never known anything different. They never told their friends, and they attended the local schools.'

Angela also spoke to the press briefly.

'This was a very challenging case and very difficult to work on,' she said. 'It was difficult for the girls to discuss it. The information came out in little bits during interviews over eight months.'

Of course, I didn't know what they said until later, when I read it in the newspapers. While they were holding this press conference Gail and I made our way to the car, but just as we got there the reporters spotted us and came running over. Paul persuaded me that perhaps I should say something. I hadn't expected this, and I had nothing prepared, but I could see it was a chance to speak out.

I simply said: 'Me and my sister have been subjected to horrific and sadistic physical and sexual abuse by the King family and others. This was a paedophile ring. Let this be a warning to others who have been named as part of this. Justice will prevail.'

As Paul and Tony were still involved with the media scrum, Gail and I jumped into a taxi and went home. I just didn't want to be there any longer. For Paul, it was a victory, for me it was not so clear-cut.

The reporters asked Paul to ask me if I would give up my anonymity and agree to have my name in the papers. It was an easy decision. I wasn't hiding. Everyone around me knew my identity, so I was happy for the whole world to know. I had travelled a long way since the day I first tentatively told Paul some of the details of my childhood, when I was terrified of anyone knowing. Now I was prepared to stand up for myself and, by doing so, to represent all victims of paedophiles.

Of course, in deciding to allow my own name to be used I couldn't speak for Heather, and so her name was never published – although I only have one sister, so everyone who knew us would know it was her.

What I didn't admit to at this stage was that Caroline Dunsmore was my mother. I was still trying to protect her, and because we had different names, I thought only the people who knew us well would realise. To me, it was still the most difficult thing to face up to. But within a few days I realised it was pointless pretending, and I allowed the press to use the fact that I was her daughter.

It never occurred to me that our case would become a worldwide story, and that everybody would know all about my past. It was the thing I had feared for so long, but when it happened, when I became the focus of so much interest, I surprised myself by coping with it much better than I would have expected. Of course, it was the fact that she was our mother that made it such a powerful story and of so much interest across the country and the world.

All my worries about Mum were eclipsed by my fear that Morris Petch was on the run. I didn't seriously think he would come looking for me, but at the back of my mind I knew that he was facing a very long sentence and might feel he had nothing to lose. My head kept going over the facts and possibilities: *I have just given evidence against this man, it's me he hates. I saw his hatred. Where is he? What's he going to do?* I just couldn't get that evil stare out of my mind.

I was also thinking that any young children he might meet were at real risk: with nothing to lose, why would he restrain himself from re-offending?

Angela tried to reassure me. 'Don't worry, we'll find him,' she said.

In fact, he was only on the loose for just over twenty-four hours: he was picked up by the police at lunchtime the next day, Saturday. Angela rang me later that day to let me know, and I felt a great sense of relief. Before his capture, his half-brother Denver Petch, the one whose appearance on my doorstep had precipitated the whole case, and who had shouted at me in the street not to involve his brother, told the press that he would not shelter Morris Petch, and would tell the police if he knew where he was.

He said that none of the family would stand by Morris Petch, and dramatically added that he hoped his brother would 'rot in hell'.

While he was missing, I didn't go anywhere without Paul. I also wanted to be sure Heather was safe, so I didn't let her out of my sight. After his arrest, he was obviously held in custody, which was a relief. His disappearance underlined all my beliefs that once found guilty of serious crimes, criminals should not be given bail before they are sentenced – not if they are guilty of terrible crimes against other human beings.

With Morris Petch behind bars, I could relax a little. But I still had to get through the next four weeks, a time when my whole life seemed to go on hold, and my complex feelings about Mum dominated almost every waking moment.

16

Those four weeks were terrible for me. It was a really hard time. I phoned Mum a couple of times, just to see if she was all right. She didn't say much, she didn't sound any different from normal. She still didn't seem to appreciate the seriousness of her situation – or, if she did, she wasn't talking about it.

One person who *was* talking was John O'Flaherty. He took advantage of his four-week freedom bonus to talk to a newspaper journalist, Alan McEwen from the *Edinburgh Evening News*, who had followed our case from the beginning, and to a radio talk-show host, Mike Graham of Talk 107, an Edinburgh station, about his crimes. Mike Graham had given plenty of air time to Paul's campaign over the previous few months, and he wanted to give the listeners the chance to hear the views of a paedophile, not to condone his behaviour in any way, but to attempt to understand it.

I'm not sure that I agree with this, although Paul does, and was instrumental in setting up the interviews.

John O'Flaherty shocked listeners and readers by the casual way in which he openly discussed what happened.

'The girls would be sitting in the living room with us like perfect little angels. Then the next minute it was like they could tell something was going to happen. It usually happened in the evening, because the girls were at school during the day. Sometimes they would be really upset afterwards and Caroline or Billy would shout at them not to say anything to anyone. I think they just got used to it after a while.'

He laid plenty of the blame on Mum.

'Caroline is making out that it was all Billy's fault now that he is dead. They were both using their daughters as little prostitutes. She is trying to play the victim when she was just as bad.'

At the same time that he was underlining her role, he was trying to downplay his own, saying that he had a 'smaller role' than many others.

'In a sense, I don't deserve to go to prison. What would that solve? People like me are ill and need treatment. I should be in hospital seeing a psychiatrist so they can learn about us paedophiles.'

But he also contributed some useful information to the debate. He said that paedophiles laugh at the Sex Offenders Register, because it doesn't work, and he said: 'If you are a paedophile you don't need to live near a school, you just need a window to look out on to the street where children pass.'

He said no member of 'the Dunsmore Gang', as he dubbed them, should ever be released back into the community, including himself – even though he didn't think jail was the appropriate place to hold them. He predicted he would get a five-year jail sentence.

I listened to the broadcast, and at the end of it the radio presenter asked him: 'Do you have anything to say to your victims?'

He said that he wanted to say sorry from the bottom of his heart. I felt a surge of anger: I don't believe he was sorry for what he did, just sorry that he was caught.

His radio talk caused an outburst of protest from listeners. The Scottish parliament Tory justice spokesman Bill Aitken described allowing him air time as 'inappropriate'. Mike Graham, who hosted the show, said he was very uncomfortable sitting in the presence of a paedophile, but, like Paul, he believed the subject was important and shouldn't be swept out of sight.

My own reaction was mixed. I had never wanted anything to do with Paul's campaigning – in fact, I had frequently asked him to stop. But I think what John O'Flaherty said on air is interesting, although it in no way lessens his crimes. He said he had always wanted to get help. However, it's easy enough to get help from your doctor if you are trying to give up smoking, but there's nothing if you are trying to stop yourself being a paedophile. He admitted that when he was in the grip of his urges, he didn't think about the children who were his victims, he didn't see them as real people. Nor did he think the Sex Offenders

Register was any kind of deterrent. He also said that he would volunteer to be chemically castrated if it would stop him having sexual feelings for children.

I'm still undecided about whether he should have been allowed to talk on air about it. I'm never happy when the name of one of my abusers is mentioned, and I don't think that hearing him talk about it will have stopped even one offence against one innocent child. Paul is sure it was a helpful contribution, but I'm not.

I felt sickened by the casual way in which John O'Flaherty could talk about such horrific events, and I very firmly believe that he deserved a long jail sentence.

John O'Flaherty's behaviour was just a slight distraction from my main preoccupation: Mum.

A couple of days before she was due in court for sentencing I phoned her and said, 'Do you want to meet up?'

'Aye,' she said.

I didn't know where she was living, but I arranged to pick her up in the centre of the city on the evening before she was due back in court. We met on the bridges ('the bridges' is what local people call North Bridge and South Bridge, which run across the mainline Edinburgh Waverley Station, right in the heart of the city). Driving to meet her felt very strange. It was a light, warm summer evening, and the pavements were busy with people making their way home from offices and shops in the city centre. The men were in shirt sleeves, the girls in bright summery dresses. Outside the pubs were knots of young people enjoying drinks in the last of the sunshine, joking and laughing together. How could they all be so happy, so normal, when something so momentous was happening in my life?

I remember seeing two girls, arm in arm, strolling along and giggling together, and I felt a deep pang of envy. Why couldn't my life be like that? Why couldn't that be me and Heather?

I spotted Mum waiting for me, her long hair loose, wearing jeans, trainers and a T-shirt, her standard uniform. She looked exactly how she always did, there was no outward sign that she was standing on a cliff edge and about to plunge over. She got into the car and we just drove around the streets for about an hour. It didn't seem appropriate to go for a drink or something to eat. I don't know where I drove, just streets, traffic lights, corners, more busy streets, looping round the city centre. The business of driving gave me something to think about, forced my thoughts on to the road and away from what lay ahead.

Neither of us knew what to say: it was too big to grasp in words. What do you say to someone who is staring a long prison sentence in the face? We made small talk.

'How is everybody?' she asked.

I told her about Dylan cutting two teeth at the same time. I told her about Jordan, who just the day before had said to me, 'Mummy, you are my number one.'

When Paul said, 'Can I be your number two?' Jordan said, 'No 'cos Dylan is my number two.'

She smiled and said, 'He's cute.'

I prattled on, trying to dredge up anything innocuous and light to keep the conversation going. But there were still long, silent pauses. Mum has never been much good at talking.

She didn't ask about Heather, nor want to see her. I asked her how she felt about the next day and she said she was scared, but it was hard to see any sign that she was. Perhaps I was too caught up with how I was feeling to really be aware of her: I was in a much more distressed state than she was.

She knew she was going to prison, but she didn't seem to have much idea what that would mean, and we never mentioned how long the sentence might be.

I remember briefly having a mad thought that I could drive away with her, keep her in the safe cocoon of the car and just drive and drive away from our lives. But it was nothing more than a fleeting thought, and after a while I began to long for the journey to end. I couldn't bear the huge emptiness between us, the sadness that neither of us could express. She was happy for our meeting to be over: she didn't press me to stay with her longer. When I dropped her off, in the same spot I had picked her up from, I stopped the car and went round to her side. I cuddled her, and told her that I loved her. She said she loved me. I know she only said it in response to me saying it, but it was the first time I had heard the words from her, apart from the occasions when I had said to her, 'You do love me, don't you?' So it was a very moving moment; she was saying the words I had always longed to hear her say. We don't normally hug each other, so that was exceptional too. She looked like she might cry, but she held back at that moment.

'Do you want me to be in court tomorrow or would you prefer it if I wasn't there?' I asked her.

'It's up to you,' she said.

'If I'm there, it will be to support you, not because I am against you,' I said.

As I drove off I looked in my driving mirror and I could see her walking slowly away in the last of the evening light. The pavement was less busy now. I could see her shoulders were shaking and her head was bowed: she was crying now. Finally, a normal reaction I could understand.

I didn't sleep that night – I wonder if she did? I went to bed at the same time as Paul and lay still for about forty-five minutes, until I could hear from his deep regular breathing that he was sound asleep. Then I slipped out of bed and went through to the living room. I didn't put any lights on, just sat there in the dark all night, while the whole household slept around me. It was a long, dark night, and I spent much of it crying, and wondering whether Mum was asleep, or whether she, too, was sitting up waiting for the dawn of the day when she would go to jail for a long time.

I decided to go to court, to see what the sentences were and to get my last look at her. I also meant what I said about supporting her: I wanted Mum to know I was there for her. All four of us – me Paul, Tony and Gail – were at the court by nine-thirty to meet Angela. We didn't see Mum or John O'Flaherty before the case, and Morris Petch was not out on bail so he was brought into the dock from the cells.

It was the first time I had seen Mum in the dock, and it was devastating. She showed no emotion. I think the shock of what was happening had made her numb to everything. In court her petite frame looked tiny against the imposing dock. I wanted to go to her, to put my arms round her. She never once looked round to see me, sitting behind and above her in the public gallery. She was wearing jeans and a pale top, not the suit she had worn during the trial.

Looking at John O'Flaherty and Mum, they appeared so ordinary, almost inoffensive. But the screen in my head threw up images from my past: the cold look on Mum's face as she watched me being abused, the way she would take the belt and strike me first and hardest, the clammy touch of John O'Flaherty's fingers.

Before sentence was passed, the defence lawyers had the chance to speak on behalf of their clients; Mum's barrister told the judge that she had suffered a life of 'horrendous abuse' herself, being raped by her father from the age of six, and by their lodger, Jamieson (he wasn't named in court but the fact that he was a convicted murderer was). He said she had had a 'deprived childhood of alcoholism, criminality and poverty'. He said she had made repeated suicide attempts, and was of very low intelligence. (The only suicide attempt I am aware of was when she had taken an overdose of paracetamol when first she came under investigation.) He also said that she was afraid of Billy, who would beat her for looking at another man or for not having his meal ready. That may have been what she told her lawyers, but it wasn't true: she and Billy rubbed along together very well; they were an unholy alliance, perfectly well suited to each other. I never heard him raise his voice to her and he was never violent towards her.

'What is the point of putting this woman in jail? She is a sinner, but she was fiercely sinned against,' said her defence counsel.

Paul was sickened by this catalogue of excuses, and he started to clap his hands in mock applause at the lawyer's skill in making a case for her. He knew he wasn't allowed to behave like that in court, so he got up and walked out, still clapping, as the court ushers came to escort him out. He simply couldn't take what he was hearing.

The judge, Lord Malcolm, then started talking to Mum. I was too distraught to take in what he was saying. I know he told her that she had committed a 'serious breach of trust on the part of a mother towards her child'.

Finally, he said: 'The sentence I give today has to mark the level of public revulsion and act as a deterrent towards others.'

Then came the two words that rang out horrifyingly clear: 'Twelve years.'

They reverberated through my head like a drumbeat. Twelve years, twelve years.

Nobody had warned me about what kind of sentence she would get, I had thought it would be five or six years, the same sort of sentence as Granddad. But twelve years?

I uttered a strangled cry and then collapsed, sobbing bitterly. Angela and Gail took my arms and half led, half carried me out. I didn't look down to see how Mum had taken the news, my eyes were blinded by tears and all I wanted to do was escape from that courtroom. Outside, after a moment on one of the benches, they led me through to the privacy of the witness room. I had wanted to hear the other sentences, but I didn't care any more, all I could think about was Mum. I was really upset, blaming myself. I kept thinking, *If I hadn't done this she wouldn't be there.*

I felt scared for her – I knew it would be tough for her in prison. I knew the other prisoners wouldn't like her because of the nature of her crimes.

Tony was the only one left in court, and he told me later that when I cried out, she turned and looked up at me, but her face showed no emotion.

From the witness room I rang Paul, who was outside on the court steps with the media. His reaction was very different from mine; he cheered, punched the air and shouted out in delight 'You fucking beauty!' Then he called to the press and TV people 'Dana's mum's got twelve years.'

I was crying, wanting him to comfort me, but his natural elation took over. I dropped the phone, really angry with him. How could he be celebrating while I felt I'd been shattered into a million lost pieces? Luckily, Gail and Angela were there to look after me.

Paul has apologised and explained since that he couldn't contain his delight when he heard that Mum was going to answer for her crimes with a long stretch in prison. As soon as he shouted out, he had a sinking feeling that he'd hurt me, and he'd instantly regretted his reaction.

I don't think anyone, not even Paul, could ever

understand the conflict of emotion that I felt. The cruellest thing about inflicting pain on your own children is that most of the time those children accept it and forgive you, just because they are your children. I don't accept it and I can't forgive Mum, but I still love her.

In the courtroom, the sentencing went on. The judge gave John O'Flaherty thirteen years, telling him, 'You have shown no real remorse or understanding of the damage caused, and your sentence should also mark public disgust at these callous crimes.'

Morris Petch's sentence was deferred for seven weeks for more background reports, but the judge warned him that he was considering imposing a life sentence. His lawyer said very little on his behalf, simply that he still claimed he was not guilty.

I wanted to wait to see Mum after the case, to tell her, 'I love you.'

Paul said the most I would get was a glimpse of a prison van, and I couldn't bear it. I didn't see Mum again on that day. But I have seen a video of her being taken out of the court building and loaded into the van, which was shown on the television news. She was wearing handcuffs, her eyes were red and puffed up, so it looked as if she had been crying. The only times I'd seen her cry before was when people had died, like Granddad King, Billy and Nana.

I was so upset that Angela arranged for me and Gail to go out of the court building by the side door again, to avoid the reporters and cameras congregated outside. There was a big crowd out there, spectators as well as the media, as many as a hundred people. I didn't feel I was in any state to talk to them. We made our way to where our car was parked, but before I could get inside the journalists saw me and came running over, cameras flashing and microphones thrust at me. I was shocked by the number of people, even more than there had been at the trial. We had been warned by the court staff, but nothing prepared me for so many of them. I wasn't frightened, but I was a bit overawed. Paul came with them, and again he persuaded me to say something to them. I hadn't thought about it beforehand, but spontaneously I said:

'Today was a great day for a victim, but a sad day for a daughter. I am happy about the sentences, but as a daughter I feel really gutted. My whole life has been hell. Going through a trial has been hell, and today has been hell.'

I was shocked by the length of Mum's sentence, but on reflection I think she should have been given life. I don't want her to have to serve more, I'm constantly worried about her in there. But when I distance myself from my love for her, I can see that her crimes were actually the worst of the three. The other two men took advantage of what was offered to them: two frightened little girls. That was grossly wrong. But she was the one making us available, and she was the person who should have been protecting us, taking care of us, making sure no harm came to us. That's what proper mothers do, and if she had been a proper mother, none of this would have happened. Our lives would have been normal, and she would not have ended up in prison.

While Paul was enjoying the moment of victory, I decided to go home in a taxi with Gail instead of waiting. I was crying all the way, and it felt as though I didn't stop crying for days. Heather had stayed home that day, and she heard the news on the radio. As I came in she ran to me and we hugged and hugged, both of us crying. Gail was doing her best to comfort us, but nothing could take the pain away.

I felt as though I was in a trance. None of the everyday things mattered. I looked after my children and the home, but I was like a robot, doing it without thinking. Paul took over most of the household jobs. I would burst into tears for the slightest reason. Heather had already told our neighbour, and as soon as she spoke to me I collapsed into sobs.

I kept thinking, *Oh my God, this is my fault. I shouldn't have told anyone.*

Everything that had felt so right about my decision to bring them to justice suddenly felt so wrong. Most of the time I blamed myself, but at other times I thought: 'Why did she put me through this? If it wasn't for her, I wouldn't be feeling like this, I wouldn't have had to stand in court, I wouldn't have seen my name all over the newspapers.'

I knew the right answers: that she deserved to go to jail, that by getting John O'Flaherty and Morris Petch off the streets I could be saving other frightened little girls, that by telling all there would be more abusers coming to justice. But none of that logic tallied with my personal feelings.

I don't really know how we survived the first few days. I couldn't focus on anything. Luckily Paul can cook, because without him we would have starved – every time I tried to prepare a meal I dissolved in tears and had to sit down. I couldn't sleep, and if I did drop off I was soon wakened by nightmares about her being murdered in jail. I couldn't eat, but Paul kept a close check on my blood sugars and kept me level on insulin.

Heather was upset too, but she recovered much more quickly than I did, distracted by the routines of her everyday life. The children picked up on my distress, of course, and they were touchingly worried about me. Little Jordan would bring me a box of tissues, and he and Ryan would cuddle me to 'make it better'. Paul, as ever, was a rock, reassuring me that I had done the right thing and being endlessly patient with me. He couldn't feel what I was going through, but he understood that I was in great pain.

The news clip of Mum being taken to prison was on the Internet, and I would call it up and watch it over and over again, mesmerised by the sight of her in handcuffs, with her long hair loose and her eyes red from crying. The photograph of her being taken to the prison van is the one that the newspapers use whenever her name comes up, as it does regularly in the Scottish press. I wish they would use a different picture of her – it upsets me all over again every time I see it.

I knew where she was. Cornton Vale is Scotland's only all-female prison, so there was nowhere else they could take her. After a week of agonising about what life was like for her in there – I knew the other prisoners would give her a rough ride as it was no secret what she'd done – I asked Tony to call the prison and to find out if she was all right.

'They say she is fine,' he told me.

It didn't make me feel better. I thought that was just

something they said to everybody, or it was Tony covering up the real truth just to make me feel better. I knew that one day she would ring me, and I was dreading it but at the same time I was desperate for the call. I was at Tony and Gail's house when it came. I didn't recognise the number on my mobile screen, but when I answered it an automated voice said, 'This call originates from a prison. If you don't wish to speak, please hang up.'

I instantly knew it was her. I felt my whole body go cold, but my heart was racing, and my breath was coming in gasps, making it difficult to speak. But it was good to know she was alive, to hear her voice. I could tell straight-away she was upset. Mum rarely shows any emotions, but her voice was trembling, as if she was on the brink of tears.

'How is it?' I asked.

'It's terrible,' she said, her voice little more than a whisper.

She couldn't tell me any more. She sounded frightened. I told her I would like to visit her, if she wanted me to. She said she did, and that she would arrange it and let me know when. She rang a couple of days later to say she had booked it, and I went to see her about two weeks after she first went inside.

Just knowing that I would see her again, that we were still in contact, made me feel slightly better. I slept properly that night, for the first time since her sentence.

17

Cornton Vale Prison is between Stirling and Bridge of Allan, about fifty miles away from where we live. It took us over an hour to get there. Tony drove, because he knew the way, and Paul came as well: I really couldn't face doing it on my own. I didn't know what I was going to find; the fact that Mum sounded frightened was something completely new to me. She had always coped with whatever life threw at her, and hearing her express any emotion at all was strange.

The first sight of the prison was very encouraging. It is not a typical huge granite or redbrick block dating back to Victorian times, the kind of prison you imagine from television and films. Instead, it looks like a series of houses set in well-tended grounds. There are bars on the windows, but they are fancy, and look ornamental, as though they have been put there to enhance the design, not to keep women in. It was built in the 1970s. It wasn't what I had expected, and it lifted my spirits. If the surroundings are good, I thought, perhaps Mum can find some sort of peace and contentment here for the next few years.

I'd been told that, with a twelve-year sentence, she would probably serve eight, as long as she behaved herself. As Cornton Vale is the only all-female prison in Scotland, it would most likely be her home for those eight years, so it is important she settles there and builds some sort of life. I know that I helped to put her there, but I think the loss of her liberty is punishment enough, and I don't want her to suffer any unnecessary extra aggravation.

Tony and Paul both came in with me. It was the first time I'd visited a prison, and I felt intimidated: it would have been much worse on my own. At the reception desk we were sent through to a waiting room, where we had to book in and show our ID. We were searched, and told that we were not allowed to take anything in with us. There were a couple of other families in there, including some children. Eventually a prison officer called out: 'Visit for Caroline Dunsmore.'

It was a closed visit, which means we saw her in a separate cubicle, not in the same room as the other prisoners have their visits. This was probably because she was in danger when mixing with the others, or perhaps it was because of the length of her sentence. Although Cornton Vale houses about 340 women, the vast majority are serving very short sentences for shoplifting or non-payment of fines. To have arrived with a twelve-year tariff, and for crimes that have been splashed across all the newspapers and television news programmes, she was bound to be notorious, and an object of great interest (and hatred) to the other prisoners.

We were taken into the cubicle where there was a table with a glass screen bisecting it. The screen was raised for us – I suppose it's a safety precaution to protect visitors if prisoners are violent or unpredictable. We sat down, and within a couple of minutes Mum came in from a door the other side of the cubicle. When I first caught sight of her, she looked different. She didn't look like Mum. She looked small, lost, frightened, frail. She was very thin, and her pupils looked tiny. I don't know what I was expecting, but when I saw her I felt very distressed, because it was clear she was finding life hard. I could feel tears welling up inside me, but I didn't cry because I didn't want to upset her. When we talked about it afterwards, Paul thought she looked normal, that there was no discernible difference. But to me she looked so helpless and terrified, out of her depth. I wanted to wrap my arms around her and tell her it would be all right.

She was wearing a prison-issue grey jumper and maroon T-shirt, but she told us she was allowed to wear her own jeans and trainers. I didn't know what to say to her, but luckily Tony is very good at making small talk, and he and Paul tried to joke and brighten things up. If it had just been her and me, I think we would have stared at each other miserably for the whole forty-five-minute visit.

The time seemed to go quite slowly. It was almost as if there was too much to say, it was hard to know where to start. She didn't say anything nasty to me, she never blamed me for putting her there. But she told us that it was really bad for her in there: the other prisoners were shouting names at her, usually 'Beast' and they threw food and sauce bottles at her. We could see bits of mashed potato, caught in her frizzy hair, from where it had been thrown at her at lunch that day. She cried and whispered, 'Please help me.'

I didn't know what to say, because I knew there was nothing I or anyone could do to help her. When it was time to go I told her I loved her, and we were both in tears.

I was very worried about her when we left. I didn't speak to Paul or Tony during the journey back to Edinburgh. I could hear them talking away, but their voices sounded distant, and nothing they said seemed to relate to me. All I could think about was Mum. I was trying to imagine what her day-to-day life was like. I sobbed and sobbed: I was suddenly very worried that she would die in there.

It was soon after this visit that she rang me from the prisoners' call box, and while we were talking on the phone I could hear other women yelling abuse at her.

'Beast!' was shouted a few times. Then one of them said: 'Who are you on the fucking phone to, Beast?'

'My daughter,' Mum replied in a small voice.

'You watch out, Beast. You've got a bleaching coming.'

I could hear them shouting it all. Mum's voice was tiny and frightened, and I realised that she was living in terror. A 'bleaching' meant that someone was intending to throw bleach over her face and into her eyes, to blind her, and I knew they meant it because she'd already had hot tea and food thrown over her.

'Why are you not under protection?' I asked her.

'They don't do that here,' she said. 'They told me I've got to mingle, get on with it.'

I felt sick and angry. Men who are convicted of serious sexual offences are well protected in prison. In Scotland they go to Peterhead Prison, which has a very large unit for sex offenders, where they are kept separate from the other prisoners. I don't think this is right: I don't think they should be allowed to mix together, sharing stories of their perversions. But I do think that any prisoner whose life and health are in danger is entitled to be protected. Justice has sent them to prison, that is their punishment. The courts decide what they deserve, not other prisoners.

I told her not to give in, to be strong.

'You don't have to explain yourself to them. You don't have to tell them anything. Stand up to them,' I said.

But I know she can't stand up to them, it's not in her nature. If it was me, I'd be saying: 'What's your problem?' Even if I was frightened, I'd put up a tough front, I wouldn't give them the victory of seeing me terrified.

But she is weak. If anyone hits her, she won't hit back. Me, I'd try hard not to let them get to me. But she doesn't have that independence, that strength. I worry that she will always be bullied in there.

I was, and am, torn apart by my feelings. I think it's right for her to be in jail because I'm hoping it will teach her a lesson. I'm hoping it will give her time to reflect on life, and to realise that what she did was wrong, and that it wasn't anybody else's fault. Every individual who took part knew what they were doing. They knew it well enough to hide it.

And she has the extra guilt to realise, because not only did she commit serious child abuse, but it was also her own daughters who were the victims. When she handed me and Heather over to those men, she had a choice. A choice to be a mother or an abuser. She made the wrong choice, and now she has to pay for it. It wasn't as if it was a one-off mistake, a lapse of judgement: she did it time after time after time. Every night when Billy took me from my bed, she knew what was happening. Every time I was taken to the House of Hell, she was part of it. She's the one who 'loaned' me and Heather to a string of dirty old paedophiles. These are very serious crimes, against the law of the land, against the laws of decency, and against every maternal instinct.

But the judge has laid down her punishment, and it should not be left to other prisoners to make it worse for her. The system in prison should protect her. I know that, given time, it should get easier for her. Myra Hindley, the most notorious British female prisoner in living memory, always had a rough ride from other prisoners whenever she moved from one jail to another, but after a few months it settled down and she was accepted. The same goes for Rosemary West, and I wish that Mum could be transferred into the English prison system where they are more geared up to long-term women offenders who have committed those kinds of crimes. I know, though, that the Scottish and English legal systems are completely separate and she will serve her time at Cornton Vale, so I want to feel she can be safe there.

After her call to me I was so angry that I rang the prison. I told the authorities that I was very worried about her, and I repeated what I had heard while she was on the phone. They reassured me that everything would be done to look after her, but I didn't feel comforted.

'Is there no way she can be put in protective custody?' I asked them.

They said they don't do that, but that they take care of all their prisoners.

I do have some sympathy with the prisoners who are aggressive towards her. I would not like to be forced to mix with someone who has committed such horrendous crimes. The world hates her, the other prisoners don't see her from the same viewpoint that I do. Most of them are in there for small crimes and, if they have children, they are probably missing them badly: it's natural they hate someone who has done such damage to her own children.

I wanted to let the other prisoners know how I felt. I wanted to appeal to them directly, to let them know that I, the daughter who had suffered the abuse, didn't want her to be attacked and treated badly. If anything happened to her, the person who would suffer the most was me, because of my terrible guilt about putting her there. So, at Paul's suggestion, I spoke to Alan McEwen at the *Edinburgh Evening News*, and he wrote a story in the paper about what was happening to her. It seemed the only way to put my views over to the other prisoners. The newspaper story quoted me:

> She's having a very difficult time. My mother deserved the sentence she received, but I still love her. Other women there have said they're going to murder her. I can hear them screaming 'Beast' when I talk to her on the phone. But I'm pleading that no one will touch her. If anything happened to Mum I would feel responsible because I put her there.

The interview was reprinted in the *Daily Mirror* and the *Daily Record.*

I also did a radio interview over the phone with a journalist about the same thing. I just hoped that the message would get through to the other women in there. Surely they would see that I, the victim, didn't want her to be attacked, and they would respect my wishes? All I wanted was for her to be left in peace.

But I don't think I helped her. The newspaper article was pushed under her cell door, and where it referred to the threat that she was going to be blinded by having bleach thrown in her eyes, someone had written next to it: 'And you are.'

She told me about this when she next phoned. It made me feel that I had wasted my time making the appeal, that it hadn't done any good. If anything, it may have drawn even more attention to her and made things worse.

As well as this, she was receiving a torrent of hate mail

from the general public: in her first two weeks in prison more than two hundred letters arrived. I can't imagine what it feels like to be at the centre of so much hatred, and she can't describe what it feels like. But I'm sure it is ever present for her.

Morris Petch was finally sentenced on 10 August 2007. Angela rang me to tell me when he was going to appear in court, and Paul and I both went. I wanted to see him go down, and I was really pleased when he got a life sentence, with a recommendation that he serve at least twelve years. This means he will be in prison longer that Mum and John O'Flaherty, and he deserves that for putting me and Heather through the trial. By trying to deny what happened he made it much worse for us, because we had to give evidence in court. Until the trial, I hated him and John O'Flaherty equally, but when he pleaded not guilty I hated him more, because he made it hard for us right to the end. Not content with abusing us when we were children, he abused us as adults by making us relive it all in front of the jury.

He was still protesting his innocence when he came up for sentence, but the judge, Lord Malcolm, said: 'It's plain from your psychological assessment that you have no remorse for these crimes or the damage caused to your victims.'

Morris Petch's lawyer told the court that she couldn't say anything in mitigation of his crimes as he was still insisting he wasn't guilty.

The judge said: 'You have been convicted of grave and disgraceful crimes against young and vulnerable children. You are in denial over your acts and your inability to control your deviant desires. It's clear from the material available to the court that you are a serious risk to the public. Nothing has been said in court on your behalf, no doubt because nothing can be said.'

He told Morris Petch that there was no guarantee that he would be released after twelve years.

'Ultimately your release date will depend upon the parole board's determination as to whether and when it is no longer necessary for the protection of the public that you should continue to be confined in prison.'

I felt a surge of elation when I heard the words 'life sentence'. Paul grabbed my hand and we turned to each other, both really pleased. There was a feeling of triumph: we had done it, we had achieved justice. It was pure happiness. I hadn't been able to feel the same about seeing John O'Flaherty go down because he came up for sentence at the same time as Mum, and any happiness I felt about his imprisonment was tinged with my sorrow for Mum.

This time, Morris Petch didn't turn and look for me in the public gallery. As he was led away, I found myself hoping that I would never see him again, ever. If he continues to deny his crimes, he will never get out of prison, and that would be fine by me.

The story was such big news that there were crowds outside the court again. We even had tourists who were in the city for the Edinburgh Festival joining the press, cameramen and spectators. Perhaps they thought the crowd had gathered for an interesting bit of street theatre! But even when the others told them 'This is the Dana Fowley case' they stayed.

I was naturally asked to comment. I said: 'I'm pleased that this particular court case has finally concluded. I am pleased with the sentence the judge has given.'

It did feel right: I hadn't realised, until Morris Petch went to jail, just how much it had been hanging over me. Now it was all over. I knew that for Mum the flurry of publicity would stir things up in the prison, but it was inevitable it would happen at some point, and she has to face a whole series of trials to come. It will be a good couple of years before Mum can hope to slide into anonymity within those prison walls.

After I had seen Mum in prison, Heather started saying she wanted to see her too, so we arranged another visit. Paul drove us there, with Jordan and Dylan in the car. He was planning to stay outside with the children, but when Heather and I went to book in for the visit, the prison officer on duty told us Heather was not on the list. She had to go outside and stay with Jordan and Dylan while Paul came in as he was still on the list. When we met Mum, she complained to the prison staff that she had definitely put her other daughter's name down for the visit, so they rechecked and Heather was able to take Paul's place in the cubicle for the closed visit.

The glass screen between us and Mum was down, and we asked if it could be raised. They told us they were short of staff, and that they were going to switch us from a closed visit to an open visit. Heather and I were shepherded back to the main reception area, and Mum was taken upstairs to the main visiting room. We were then called in again.

In this room there were tables dotted about, with chairs around them, and vending machines against the wall to provide hot and cold drinks, crisps, chocolate bars etc. Mum wanted coffee and crisps. It was much more civilised than the closed visit: it felt more normal, more relaxed, and we could talk more casually. The closed visit had been much more intense, partly, I guess, because it was my first one.

There were only two other prisoners having visits, so there was no trouble. I think they were remand prisoners, so they probably didn't know who she was.

The first thing we noticed when we saw her was that she had had her hair cut. She always had very long, frizzy-curly hair, but it had been cut at the prison hairdresser's. Apparently they had spent ages straightening it, and I expect it had looked nice when it was first done. But back in her cell, without hair straighteners, it had gone back to being frizzy, and it just looked a mess. She was pleased with it, so I told her it looked great.

Despite all the confusion and time wasting at the beginning of the visit, we were not allowed any extra time, and the forty-five minutes seemed to be over very quickly. Before we left, both Heather and I hugged her, but this time she didn't cry. I'm glad about that, because I think

Heather found the visit very stressful, not so much because of Mum but more because of the whole security procedures of the prison. She was frightened by it all, and she has never asked to go back.

This time I left twenty pounds for Mum. She didn't ask for it, but I know she needs money to buy phonecards and small luxuries like shampoo.

Soon after this visit, Mum tried to kill herself. She jammed a towel in the top of the door and tried to hang herself with a makeshift noose, made from the towel. According to her, prison officers had to force their way into the cell to save her, and she was taken to a special cell for suicide-risk prisoners, where she was stripped of everything that could possibly be used to kill herself with.

She rang me and her first words were, 'I tried to kill myself.'

'How did you do that?' I asked, shocked that there would be any way of committing suicide in there, and she described it. I was very upset. 'Don't be silly, don't do anything to hurt yourself. You've just got to accept that you are where you are. It will get easier. Look to the future – you'll be out one day,' I said.

There's never any time on the phone to really talk. After a minute or so she says, 'My money's running out, I've got to go.'

I'm not sure that I believe she wanted to kill herself, but I think she wanted to draw attention to how bad it was in there for her, and how she needed more protection. It misfired: according to her, the prison staff are largely unsympathetic and share the same view of her as the prisoners. She claims one of them said: 'Why the fuck didn't you do this outside and save us a lot of hassle in here?'

If that's true, it's very wrong that they treat her like that. They are supposed to be professionals. They should be there for the care and welfare of the prisoners, no matter who they are and what crimes they have committed. One of them was quoted in a newspaper saying, 'I couldn't believe it when I saw Dana visit her mum.' I'm shocked that they make comments like that: it's nothing to do with them. When I rang up to complain, another officer said to Mum: 'Your daughter's been on the phone causing havoc.'

They can create problems in subtle ways. At one time, when Mum was applying for a visit, she was repeatedly told that all the visit slots were full. It was only after she complained to a governor that she got the visit dates.

So I despair of being able to help her at all.

The third time I went to see her, again Paul came with me. It was a closed visit. This time she was covered in scratches on her arms, as if someone had grabbed her, and she had been burnt; it was a very small burn which could have come from a cigarette. Again, she looked very sad and frightened, and I was very worried about her. My mum is now as vulnerable as I was as a child. I know she turned her back on me then, but I can't turn my back on her now. Two wrongs don't make a right. I feel a huge responsibility for her.

The good news is that she has been moved to another section of the prison. Cornton Vale is a series of five blocks, known as 'halls'. These are subdivided into six-or seven-room units, each with its own dining-cum-sitting room, and most of them with a kitchen. Mum was initially held in Ross Hall, which is mainly full of remand prisoners, and where she had to work in the laundry, which probably left her exposed to attacks. She has now been transferred to Bruce Hall, where the long-term offenders are held, and she is beginning to look and sound a bit better.

Although you may think that prisoners serving long sentences have nothing to lose by attacking someone like her, in fact, the experience of most of the prison service is that the prisoners who are in for many years are more settled, and more intent on not rocking the boat than the short-term offenders. She has even told us that she has made a friend, a woman who is in prison for seven years for suffocating her baby daughter, twenty-four years earlier. They are the same age, both serving long sentences, and both of them reviled and hated by the other prisoners. I am glad, at least, that she has someone to sit with and talk to.

I'm sure there will be a fresh round of attacks when it all comes up in the news again, when the others come to trial – especially as she is giving evidence against them. She will have to be prepared for that, and I hope the prison authorities are prepared as well, and manage to protect her more effectively,

She phones me, probably once or twice a week, but there is no set pattern. The conversations don't vary greatly: she asks after everyone, and I tell her any snippets of news I have about the children. She never asks about them individually, and she never asks about Heather. The calls are very brief, because she phones my mobile which eats up the units on her phonecards. But I am always relieved to hear from her, to know that she is all right.

I also get a bit of feedback from Angela, who has been to the prison to interview Mum about her evidence against the men coming up in the next trials. I texted Angela after she went recently and asked, 'How is she?'

Angela replied that she was fine. I wasn't completely reassured: Angela wouldn't tell me anything that would worry me.

My recent visits have been open visits and there have been no unpleasant incidents. It's only me and Paul who go, and we have the same stilted conversations.

'Are the bairns all right?' she always asks.

I tell her all the news about Dylan starting to walk and talk, what Jordan's been doing now he's at nursery school and anything else I can think of to make the time pass. I always ask how she is, and on these recent visits she seems better, more settled.

I think my visits to her will probably tail off. At first I just wanted to see her, make it up to her. But now, as distance gives the trial and its aftermath a little bit more perspective, I find it harder and harder to understand her. There are times when I think, 'Bugger you, you didn't care about me then and you don't care about me now.'

Twice Paul and I have actually been in the car driving to

the prison when I have told him, 'Turn back. Fuck her. She's a bastard. I don't want to see her.'

When we have got home, she has rung, as expected, and I haven't answered my mobile, getting Heather to tell her I'm not in. I can't face the disappointment in her voice, or the guilt it creates in me. I picture her all pleased because she's having a visit, and then being told that nobody has come. This image eats away at me.

At other times I don't feel so angry, but visiting her seems like a huge waste of my life. It takes over an hour each way to get there, we have to be there half an hour early, and then we only get to see her for forty-five minutes. That is half a day gone: it's time when I could be in the park with my children, or taking them out for something to eat.

She'll be nice to me now, because she needs me. Why couldn't she have been like this in the first place? She's even said sorry to me.

'I deserve to be in jail for what I've done,' she told me.

But she should never have put herself into a position where she has to say sorry. If she'd behaved like a mum – not even a particularly good mum, but an adequate mum – none of us would be in the position we are in today.

Since she's been in prison she says she loves me and misses me. If only she knew how much, in my earlier life, I longed to hear her say those words. But now I'm cynical, I think she's saying it because it means I will help her.

I told her before she went to prison that I was the only person who really cares about her. She's spent all her life giving top priority to the men in her life, above her children. She thought they were the most important people. But where are they now? I told her to wake up to the fact that me and Heather are all she has, and I'm the only one in a position to care for her and look after her. The men have all gone, but I'm still here. That's why she is being nice to me.

Christmas was hard, knowing that she was in there. Ever since Paul and I set up home together, we have always laid on a good Christmas, and until the final two years, when she was under the police investigation, Mum always spent it with us. Even those two years she was not with us, at least I knew she was free and enjoying Christmas somewhere. But last Christmas I knew she was in prison, and it felt really strange.

18

My journey is not over yet, it will be a long time before I can truly say I have the one thing I have always wanted, more than anything: a normal life. There is more disruption to come with the forthcoming court cases, and there is a great deal of work needed to stabilise my family and to get our lives on an even keel. But now that I am not living a lie any more, now that the worst of the trials is over, I'm optimistic and looking forward to a better and quieter life.

The police and Procurator Fiscal have asked me if I feel strong enough to go ahead with the prosecutions that are coming up. To me, it's a piece of cake after going into court against my own mother. Now all I am being asked to do is give evidence against some of the disgusting men who abused me and Heather, and I won't have a problem. I will rejoice to give evidence against them. What is the worst thing their clever lawyers can do? Call me a liar, like Morris

Petch's counsel did? Well, I'm not lying, and I can't be tripped up because everything I say is the truth.

But until all the trials are over, appointments for interviews with the police, the lawyers, and dates to go to court still dominate my diary.

I do worry about Heather having to give evidence again, and I don't believe she should have to. Heather gets very distressed, even though she gets over it quite quickly. She deserves enormous credit for what she has already done in court, giving evidence against Morris Petch.

Today, Heather goes to college three days a week, and she has a voluntary job in a café. She started college in 2006, in the middle of the police investigations. Her social worker found the course for her, and it has proved a godsend.

At college she learns useful skills, such as how to cook and how to manage her life. She loves it there, and every term she takes on new courses. She's very happy. At the end of each course she gets certificates to show she has passed, and Paul and I always go to her prize-giving events. She's really proud of herself, and we're really proud of her. When she goes up on the platform to get her certificate she always looks round to make sure we are watching, and Paul and I clap like mad.

She has blossomed since she has lived with us. She has friends, her own life, and a secure home. Every few weeks we have a care meeting to discuss Heather's progress, with her social worker, her psychiatrist, her diabetic nurse and everyone else who is concerned about her welfare, and everyone says how well she is doing. She won't hear of living anywhere else: she doesn't want to live independently, even though her social workers have suggested she can manage it.

As for us, we can't imagine not having Heather with us. She's like another of our children. If I buy a sweet for the little ones, I always have to buy one for Heather. When they got pocket Nintendos, Heather had to have one too. Then, just like a small child, she pestered and pestered me for a game she wanted. At Christmas she has to have exactly the same number of presents as the children. And if we eat at McDonalds, Heather has a Happy Meal.

I have to supervise her doing her insulin injections. She has to inject twice a day, and she's capable of doing it, and being responsible for it. But she has a habit of missing the injections. On a couple of occasions she has had to be rushed to the high-dependency unit at the hospital because she has missed her jabs.

The most important thing with Heather is to constantly tell her you love her, that she's special. She craves attention, and to get it she'll miss her insulin and end up in hospital. I get cross with her, because she knows what she's doing. But at the same time, I understand: she lacked so much love as a child she now needs constant reassurance that we do all love and care for her.

At the moment she has a boyfriend, someone she met at college. It's very innocent and sweet. When it was her birthday he bought her presents, and they went out for a meal. Even Jordan is very protective of her.

'Have you been kissing my Auntie Heather?' he asked, when her new boyfriend came home the first time.

I always dreamed of having children, and giving them the childhood I never had. I wanted them to be loved, looked after, treated right, sleeping safe in their beds at night, with nothing to hurt them. Although our family life has been very disrupted by everything that has happened, I hope I have achieved this.

As you can probably imagine, I very rarely let anyone look after my children. The only people I trust to babysit are Tony and Gail, Brenda and Bilko, and Young Paul. Heather, too, is very capable of caring for them for a few hours: she loves it, and the children love her too. I'm still naturally distrustful of anyone outside this small group, and the events with Tam, have only made me more so.

Also, because of Mum's involvement, I know that women are not necessarily trustworthy either. I think women who abuse children are very rare, but experience has taught me that I should never think anyone incapable of it. Nobody from outside would ever have suspected my mum.

So I have probably been over-protective towards my children, especially Jordan, my firstborn. Abuse doesn't stop with the abuser and the victim. The fallout is massive. We have tried never to speak about it in front of our children, but inevitably they have heard things. They have seen me sad and upset, they know that I have been rushed to hospital when the stress was too much for me.

Jordan's childhood has been seriously disrupted by what

has gone on. He has never really had the normal routines of infancy, and he is so close to me and Paul that he suffers from real separation anxiety unless he is with one of us.

He found it very hard to settle at nursery school because he had hardly ever been apart from me or Paul. I found it difficult letting him go, too. For many weeks, one of us had to stay with him: Heather did it on Mondays and Tuesdays, the days she is not in college, and I stayed with him the rest of the week. Even when I was there, he panicked if I was out of his sight. It was hard work, because there was Dylan to take care of, too.

Jordan is so used to Angela Edmunds being at our home that he regards her almost as one of the family, but he is very suspicious of uniformed police and of ambulance men. He has seen me taken to hospital by ambulance so many times that if he sees an ambulance near our home he screams, 'Don't take my mummy. Don't go away, Mummy.' He's also always anxious when Paul goes out. 'Take me with you, Daddy,' he pleads. He's a very loving, affectionate little boy, but he is also very boisterous and, because I have tended to give in to him to make up for everything, he's not used to any discipline.

Dylan is different. He settled into a routine straightaway. He plays happily in his cot when he is put to bed, then sleeps well and, if he wakes early, plays with his toys until I get him up for breakfast. As a baby he only cried if he needed feeding or changing, and as a toddler he is sturdy and cheerful, small for his age but chunky. Perhaps he is more settled because he is my second child, and I am more experienced, but I also think it's because he's too young to have been affected in the same way Jordan has by what is going on in our lives.

I feel horrified when I look at Jordan now, and I realise that he's only a few months younger than I was when the abuse started. It really brings it home to me how small and vulnerable I was. Other things upset me, too: if my children fall over, I run to pick them up and comfort them. It's something I never experienced in my own childhood, and it's the lack of those little caring gestures that hurts me almost as much as the appalling abuse.

Every day of my life I tell my children that I love them, and they say it back to me. They have been brought up knowing love, and how to express it. It affected my life very badly that no one told me they loved me, and it will never happen to my children.

When we are sitting watching television, Jordan snuggles in between me and Paul for cuddles, and in the mornings he jumps into bed next to me. I could never have done that as a child. The only time I ever went to my mother's bed was to be abused, apart from Christmas morning when we opened some of our parcels there.

I always knew that what happened to me was wrong, but having my own children has made me acutely aware of just how appalling it was. I don't know how I learned to be a good mother: they say you learn to be a parent from your own parents. That's the excuse that so many abusers use: they were abused themselves, so they learned to abuse. But I'm proof that you don't have to follow your parents, and I believe there are many more victims like me who have never been tempted to become abusers themselves, and who have struggled away from the terrors of their own childhood to become good and loving parents to their own children.

Young Paul has also been quite deeply affected by everything. He is close to me, and to Heather – they squabble like brother and sister, but in the end he is very fond of her. He has heard a lot of things that upset him, and he has witnessed a great deal, including the two women who rampaged through our home, while an angry crowd fought outside.

He has a very mature head on his young shoulders. There have been times, especially in the run-up to the court case, when I have been in bits, and he has cuddled me and said, 'It's all right, we're all here to look after you.'

He's a bright lad, but since he left school he hasn't been able to find work. He has had a long-term relationship with a girlfriend who gave birth to a baby son, another Paul, but unfortunately they split up soon after the birth, which has broken Young Paul's heart. He keeps in touch with his son, but is desperate to spend more time with him.

Ryan doesn't really understand what has happened, but he says things like, 'I hate those people for what they have done to my mum.' He struggles at school, and he is easily bullied. He is big for his age – already taller than me – and it's heartbreaking to see younger kids taking advantage of him. He's a kind-hearted, loving boy, and both Paul and I are really worried that when he goes to high school he will find it very difficult to cope. We feel he should be in a special school, where he will get an education tailored to his needs.

I would like to have another baby: I would love to have a little girl, to show her the childhood I never had. But if I never manage to have a daughter, I will be content with the lovely boys I already have. I don't want to have another baby until our lives are really settled, and that won't be until all the trials and the police investigation are completely finished. I know that, with my health problems, another pregnancy will most likely be difficult, but I'm happy to take that chance.

A couple of years ago, when Heather started college, I decided to go, too. I wanted to do an access to nursing course, going back to my very first career choice, to qualify as a nurse. But the course was full, so I enrolled in another one, to study complementary therapies. I only managed to go for three months or so, because I became ill, then my time was so taken up with the police inquiry, and then I became pregnant with Dylan.

I started the course because I desperately needed something else to be happening in my life, apart from talking about the abuse. I wanted to go to college where nobody would know my background, where I would be just like one of the other students. I've changed my mind about nursing because recently I've spent so much time in hospital that I don't ever want to go inside one again, certainly not to work. Perhaps one day I'll go back to studying, but for now I don't want to be away from my children for long. They will only be little once, and I, more than anybody, know how important it is to cherish their childhood.

When we finally get settled, and the last of the trials is out of the way, I'm sure Paul and I will both find jobs, and get our lives back to normal.

Paul has been my anchor for many years now. Whenever I have wavered, whenever I am overwhelmed by grief, he reminds me that I have done right, that I have put dangerous paedophiles behind bars, that I have shed light on crimes that so often go unpunished, undiscovered, and leave many victims damaged for life.

This paedophile ring, these people who stole my childhood, would have got away with it if it hadn't been for Paul. I may have had the evidence, but it was Paul who gave me the drive and the strength to go through with it.

There are critics who say Paul became a fanatic. But I can see that it gave him an outlet for his anger. His partner, the woman he loved, had been repeatedly raped by the biggest paedophile gang in Britain, and he somehow had to deal with that. He found it very hard to push away the image of me as a small child, frigid with fear, waiting to be taken from my bed to be raped. It plagued him and he had to do something to make amends for the past he couldn't protect me from.

Paul can speak for himself, though. This is how he feels about me and my past:

'Finding out what happened to Dana never threatened my love for her. I can't understand men who leave their partners when they find out they have been raped or abused. A body is just a body: what you fall in love with is the person inside the body. People, men mainly, actually ask me: "How do you feel sleeping with her after all those blokes had sex with her?"

'I tell them what I tell Dana, and what I feel: every time I touch her, it is with love. Nobody ever touched her with love before me. She was a love virgin when I met her, and I am the only *lover* she has ever had.

'I was very lucky because my children found a wonderful mother figure in Dana. She treats Ryan the same way that she treats Jordan and Dylan, and she loves them the same. Sometimes, when I'm telling Ryan off, she will take his side. She's full of love. It's as if she got all the love that was going in her family, the full quota.

'Everything she has been through has made Dana very strong. Before the trial, I was really worried about her state of mind. She tried to kill herself twice, and I could understand why. But now I know that she won't do that again. Her worst fears are over, she's faced the world and been open about her past. She was terrified of being known as "the lassie who was abused". Well, now everyone knows, and she has found that a source of strength. She has realised that people don't think badly of her; they admire her for having the strength to tackle her abusers. Now she's "the lassie who kicked ass".'

Paul and I get on better than ever nowadays. There are still some frictions, the main one being that he uses the abuse to excuse everything I do or say. If I'm stroppy or difficult, he'll always try to justify it by saying, 'It's OK, I know what you've been through.'

I tell him that being abused isn't everything in my life, I don't want it to be an excuse. If I'm difficult and say nasty things to him occasionally, he shouldn't be so tolerant. He's too understanding. I tell him, 'I was abused, but I'm not being abused any more. That's in the past. How I behave now is down to me, there are no excuses. I'm not the scared wee lassie I was then. I've grown up.'

I don't want to spend my life being judged by what happened to me as a child. The last thing I want is pity. I hate the idea of people feeling sorry for me. That was one of my greatest worries about it all coming out. Not only would it be shameful, but people would also pity me. I am a strong, independent person, and that's how I want people to see me.

My health is still poor. I seem to have very low resistance to infections, probably because my whole immune system is under attack both from my liver problems and my diabetes, and also from stress. I am often sick, I lose weight even though I try hard not to, I am constantly having to take antibiotics for a whole series of infections, and I still have to spend time in hospital.

My hope is that when the rest of the court cases are over, when we have settled into a new home away from the memories, when the children are all happy at school and I have achieved my life's ambition to be part of an ordinary family, my health will also improve. Stress plays a big part in the imbalance in my blood sugars; it probably plays a big part in my general debility too.

Since my mum's court case made headlines, we have had many letters of support. Among them have been several from other victims. Most of them will probably never have the courage – or the evidence – to see their abusers behind bars, but some will. One girl wrote to me: 'If you can tell about your mother, I can tell about my father.'

I hope my experience, and the publicity it has had, will make a difference, will encourage others to talk. I want to say to victims: don't worry, be brave.

I always feared that if anybody found out about my background it would destroy me, but, on the contrary, the publicity has made me strong. I knew that what I had done was right, but now that has been confirmed by the public reaction.

Luckily for me, I have a tight family unit with Paul and the children, and Paul's family have accepted me. Otherwise I would have no family apart from Auntie Brenda and Uncle Bilko and their girls, who are still very much part of our lives.

I know that one day Mum will be out. She will probably serve eight years, if she behaves in prison – and I can't imagine her not behaving. She will only be fifty-one, not very old at all. I hope she will have learned some very big lessons, but, as Paul says, in some ways Mum is like a grenade waiting to go off. If nobody pulls the pin, she'll be fine. But if she hooks up with another man who is into child abuse, I think she would be capable of doing it again.

She told Paul and me that the reason she is giving evidence in the other trials is so that when she comes out we can all be friends again. But that's not a good reason, it's self-serving. She should be doing it because she recognises that what they did is very wrong, and they deserve punishment.

I try not to think about what will happen when she comes out. Most victims of abuse worry about when their abusers will be released and that they will come looking for them: in my case, I know Mum will expect me to be there for her. It is such a high-profile case, that I'm sure when she does come out it will all be in the newspapers yet again, and life will be difficult, not just for her but also for us. I think I will probably agree to see her, but it will be on my own: I won't be inviting her in to my family home, or letting her see my children. That's not because I think she would abuse them, but I'm not prepared to take any risks, and she gave up the right to be a part of my family a long time ago.

I hope when she comes out she'll be more prepared to live a decent, normal life.

19

'How could she?' is the question I have heard, over and over again. It is a question I have asked myself many times. I have no answer. I accept no excuses, and my mum doesn't make any. If I was in her position, I would probably be trying to shift a lot of the blame on to Billy, as her lawyer did in court. But she doesn't say anything about it, and I don't ask because I know the only answer I would get from her is: 'I don't know.'

When I was a child, I thought what was happening to me was normal at first. That it happened in all families. When I grew older I realised it was wrong and I was deeply ashamed of it, even though I was an innocent victim. I went to the other extreme: I felt that we, me and Heather, were the only children in the whole world who were suffering such chronic abuse.

Today, I know that paedophilia is widespread and there

are many, many victims. We are moving in the right direction: more and more is coming out, children are being listened to, there are a few (nowhere near enough) support systems to help victims. It's not being swept under the carpet as it once was, but we are a long way short of really dealing with it.

My case would have been at the extreme end of the scale by any standards: I suffered abuse for ten years. Heather's abuse lasted even longer. What makes our story different, and even more horrific, was the involvement of our mother.

If Mum hadn't been part of it, I would be able to move on from my past much more easily. The fact that when I was a child I could never talk to her is the bit that makes it most difficult. Even if it had taken all this time to come out, just having a mum to talk to and trust, to hug me when I most needed it, would have helped me a great deal through these difficult years.

As you will have gathered reading this book, I have very mixed feelings towards her. I'm confused about how I feel. Sometimes I see her as a frightened woman of low intelligence, and I feel sorry for her. At other times, I remember her whipping me, encouraging others to hurt me, joining in orgies of sexual abuse in which I was available to be attacked and humiliated as much as anyone wanted. I clearly remember that she wasn't held hostage in those terrible situations: she stayed there of her own free will. She could have taken us to school one day and carried on walking straight to the nearest police station, and put a stop to everything that was happening.

How can I ever reconcile those two images? I don't suppose I ever will. All I know is that I am very different from both my parents. I don't know where I got my strength, my independence and my sense of right and wrong: but I know it wasn't from either of them.

My reactions are so different from my mum's. When I see her upset and scared, I want to protect her and help her. She saw me frightened and upset many, many times when I was a child, but no protective instinct kicked in with her. She's still my mother but I don't think I have ever been her daughter.

My sons are mine: if they cry because something has hurt them, I feel sad. I want their lives to be as perfect as I can make them. Mum never felt like that about me and Heather. What was going on in her head when it was all happening? I'd really love to know, so that perhaps I could start to understand.

We will never sit down together and talk about it properly, but there are questions I would love to ask her. I want to know how Billy first told her he had abused her five-year-old daughter, and then asked her to join in. I'm sure he would have known that she had been abused by her own father, and that she would consequently accept child abuse more readily than someone who had never experienced it. But I'm still puzzled as to how he told her, and how she reacted. Obviously, he gauged her right: she didn't object.

How could they then say to the others who joined in: 'Would you like to rape Dana?' How did that conversation come about? How did these paedophiles recognise each other? Remember, this was before the anonymous cloak of Internet chat rooms.

They took risks, involving so many other people. Any one of them could have gone to the police. But I'm sure that they never thought the wee lassie they raped so long ago would one day be strong enough to stand up and point a finger at them. It must have come as a complete shock.

I suspect there were many other victims of the men who abused me: I know John O'Flaherty says I was gang raped several times, but I have only one memory. What chills me is that he's probably right that there were other gang rapes, but doesn't recall enough about his victims – to him and the others they were nothing more than pieces of meat – to remember that it wasn't me all those times.

I tolerate no excuses for them. Mum is of low intelligence, but Billy wasn't. And they all knew the difference between right and wrong: they knew their deeds had to be hidden, and we had to be brainwashed into not telling.

Most of all, the quest that has dominated much of my life is to see evidence that my mother loves me. She never once told me as a child that she loved me. I'd be shocked if my sons had to ask me if I loved them.

Now that she's in prison she can say she loves me, but it's for her own sake, not mine. She is saying what I want to hear because she needs me to visit her, she has no other friends. I just want what any child would want: to be loved by their mother. If you have that love, you might easily take it for granted. If you don't have it, the lack haunts your whole life.

To my mother, nothing mattered apart from the

pleasure of whichever man was in her life at the time. Her man, whoever it was, came way above her children. I don't think she would ever have initiated the abuse against us, but meeting Billy and his family meant she would do anything for them, and that involved treating us as though we were her property, without feelings of our own. She knew we were suffering, she heard me cry out many times for her help. But she was unmoved.

So my feelings towards Mum are very confused, very difficult. I veer between loving her and hating her. The more I think about what she did, the more I hate her, and perhaps that's the way it will continue, so that eventually I can stand back from her and say dispassionately, 'I never want to see you again.'

Right now, however, I still love my mum, and I can't help it. I wasn't born with the same feelings as she was, the same coldness that she has. I know that if the positions were reversed, she could turn her back and say 'I'm having nothing to do with you.' But I can't. It would be like water off a duck's back to her, but for me it is very, very hard.

Since I've grown up, it's as if we have swapped official mother – daughter roles: she's the one who needs looking after and I've become the one who looks after her, despite the fact she never did that for me. I've had to do everything for myself in life, I've never had her to lean on. I love her in the way you love a child, and at times I think: 'It doesn't matter what she did, she's still my mum, and everybody needs a mum.'

Even now, I feel guilty about what I have done, giving evidence against her. I wish she was out here, I wish I could see her on a normal basis, not have to visit her in prison. At times I feel like a naughty child who should not have told tales. The deep brainwashing of my childhood, the message that was drilled into me that I should never tell anyone, still holds some sway over me in dark moments even though rationally I know I did the right thing.

I have never had any organised counselling for what I have been through. After the trial Angela took me along to meet a counsellor from Victim Support, but I knew within a few minutes of being left with her that I wasn't going to benefit from talking it all through with her: I'd been through it so much for the police. All I would achieve would be to relive it just so that somebody could tell me it was all right to have the confused feelings I have.

But I have had unofficial counselling, and it has been invaluable. Paul has counselled me, Angela has counselled me. Very importantly, I have found a great friend, ally and counsellor in Shy Keenan, who, with Sara Payne (the mother of the murdered girl Sarah Payne), has set up a support and advocacy system for abuse victims, The Phoenix Chief Advocates.

Shy rang me soon after Mum's trial was over, and after my name had appeared across the newspapers and television screens of Britain. Shy herself has been through so much: she was abused throughout her childhood, sold to other men by her stepfather, and the abuse was filmed and, years later, posted on the Internet. She worked hard to collect evidence against her stepfather, and eventually saw him go to jail for fifteen years. This was more than twenty years after she had escaped from his clutches. So her story parallels mine in so many ways.

It is tremendously good for me, being able to talk to her. Paul and Angela are brilliant, but Shy is the only one who really understands the frightened little girl I once was, because she has been there. More importantly, she understands the strong woman I now am, because she is there, too. In 2003, her campaigning was recognised when she went to 10 Downing Street to meet Cherie Blair and to be awarded the title of Britain's Children's Champion, an award set up jointly by the charity Barnardo's, the *News of the World*, and the Marriott hotel chain.

Shy and Sara Payne aim to set up a retreat where victims of abuse can go, somewhere they can feel completely safe and relaxed while being counselled. For more information on the brilliant work they do, visit their website: www.phoenixsurvivors.com.

I can ring Shy any time, and in the aftermath of the trial, whenever I felt I was drowning she reached me, grabbed my hand and pulled me back to the surface. When I was in pieces, I spoke to her every day, sometimes for hours. I can tell her, much more easily than I can tell Paul, just how much I miss my mother and how I am so torn apart by my love for her and my hatred for what she did. The really important thing is that we have become friends. We usually end up having a laugh together: I can talk to her about other things, not just the abuse and the trials. A sad conversation usually ends up being a normal chat between two good friends.

We have never met face to face, although I am sure we will – but I feel as though I know her so well. I have been intending to make time to go down to England to meet her, but my family life is very busy. Shy wants me to train to help other victims of abuse, and I can see that as a good way forward. If I can extend my hand and pull one other drowning victim to the surface, as Shy has done for me, it will all have been worthwhile.

I worry that my confused feelings about Mum will hamper me as a counsellor. I condemn all paedophilia, so I can't really make an exception and say that I still love my mother, who is a paedophile. But I'm hoping that my feelings will become clearer the more I distance myself from the legal processes, which are still ongoing. When all the trials are over, I hope I will be able to look at everything, including my mother's role, from a clearer perspective.

The other great therapy for me has come with writing this book. I wanted to do it: I wanted to give my own children a full and accurate record of what my life has been like. After all, Jordan and Dylan will one day have to face the facts that their great grandfather, their grandfather, their grandmother and many of their mother's stepfamily are paedophiles. My whole rotten family, in fact, with only a few exceptions, are classed as paedophiles.

So I need to show my sons that it is possible to step away from it. I don't want them to think I did nothing. Most of all I want them, and all children everywhere, to believe that it is OK to tell if any adult is abusing you. I don't want any other child to feel they have to hold it inside for many years, like I did. Children need to know that you can stand up and do something, and people will believe you and help you. This book is for them: it is my record of what I went through as a child and what I went through again, as an adult, to get justice.

I can't honestly say that we will ever be able to stop paedophilia. How can we ever know what goes on behind every closed door? But we can control it and reduce it by putting fear into the abusers, fear that they will go to prison for very long sentences when their crimes are uncovered. We need to tell them: 'If you get caught, this is what will happen to you. And you will get caught, because we will listen to children, and we will believe what they are saying.'

I'm not idealistic enough to think that the prospect of a long jail sentence will stop them at the moment that they are in the grip of their urge to abuse, but I think that the threat of punishment and condemnation by the whole of society will help to contain and reduce their crimes.

If by making my own story so public I can help put in place support for other victims, so that they will not go through the terror I experienced, that will be a great reward for everything I have gone through.

If I had known how hard these last few years would be, would I have done it? After all, apart from my huge black secret, my life was pretty near perfect.

The honest answer is that I don't know. We have walked to the gates of hell and back since the truth began to come out. Our lives have been turned upside down. Paul and I have weathered some big crises in our own relationship.

The paedophiles who blighted my childhood can still get into my life and tear it apart – perhaps that is a victory for them. They had power over me as a child and my adult life is still under threat because of what they did to me.

All the time that I spent with the police and the Procurator Fiscal was time away from my children. Now I dread going into a newspaper shop, because my face is so often across the front page: every time something happens to Mum in jail, the same pictures of me are used.

But to offset all that, I, too, have my victory. I have seen the perpetrators go to jail. I have seen justice at work, and I have felt a deep sense of triumph because, although I can't right the wrongs of my childhood, I can at least make those who caused them pay.

But, most importantly, I know that now my abusers are locked up they can't hurt my children or any other childen. The cycle of abuse stops here and that's what really counts.

Acknowledgements

The greatest thanks go to my partner Paul, for supporting me through this whole ordeal and for loving me.

I would also like to thank:

My stepson Young Paul, who also stood right beside me through all my court cases, and my stepson Ryan, who helped me through my sadness with his cuddles.

My two kids Jordan and Dylan, for giving life meaning.

My sister Heather, for surviving her ordeal and speaking up.

And my other family members and friends who have supported me.

The police officers who helped bring my abusers to justice: Callum Lamond and, most importantly, Angela Edmunds, who has been a great support through this whole ordeal.

Shy Keenan who, when I felt I was drowning, took my hand and pulled me back to the surface.

Susan Smith my agent.

Emma Rose a great publisher.

And finally, but with ever-lasting appreciation, Jean Ritchie for helping me tell my story.